DEATH ON THE TRACKS

PAUL WESTMORELAND

PUFFIN

PUFFIN BOOKS

UK | USA | Canada | Ireland | Australia
India | New Zealand | South Africa

Puffin Books is part of the Penguin Random House group of companies
whose addresses can be found at global.penguinrandomhouse.com

www.penguin.co.uk www.puffin.co.uk www.ladybird.co.uk

Penguin Random House UK

First published 2024
001

Set by Dynamo Limited
Printed in Great Britain by Clays Ltd, Elcograf S.p.A.

The authorized representative in the EEA is Penguin Random House Ireland,
Morrison Chambers, 32 Nassau Street, Dublin D02 YH68

A CIP catalogue record for this book is available from the British Library

ISBN: 978–0–241–72340–1

All correspondence to:
Puffin Books
Penguin Random House Children's
One Embassy Gardens, 8 Viaduct Gardens, London SW11 7BW

FSC www.fsc.org MIX Paper | Supporting responsible forestry FSC® C018179

Penguin Random House is committed to a sustainable future for our business, our readers and our planet. This book is made from Forest Stewardship Council® certified paper.

This book is dedicated to my dearest friend Shazir,
and all the adventures we had travelling the world.

HOW TO USE THIS BOOK

This book contains three stories, several mysterious murders and dozens of fiendish puzzles.

But the Murder Puzzle Mysteries are unlike other books. You can't simply read them from one chapter to the next.

Instead, you must solve the puzzles. How you solve them will determine where you turn next. Along the way, you'll discover clues, find pieces of evidence and uncover the truths lurking behind the mysteries. You might even catch a killer!

But be careful: the path you take through a maze, the differences you spot, the wire you cut to defuse a bomb – each puzzle you succeed with will take you closer to catching the killer!

Don't be afraid, though. Everything you need to guide you is contained within the pages of the story. The objective of each puzzle and what you need to do will be explained. Some puzzles are straight-forward, while others rely on clues within the story and will require some deduction – it wouldn't be a detective story without a bit of deduction, now, would it?

So read everything carefully and keep a close eye on the details. If something doesn't make sense, don't worry – I assure you all the information you need is right there. And you always can check your answers against the solutions at the back.

Your goal is to find your way to the star endings. But if the worst happens and you come to a dead end, simply go back to a puzzle and try again.

Whatever you do, don't give up . . . or let the murderers get away!

INTRODUCTION

By the time Oxford professor Peter Hamatum-Sizzle inherited his family's vast fortune, he was too old to enjoy it. He'd always dreamed of travelling the world and the hours he'd spent in his study imagining where he'd go and what he might see were beyond estimation.

But alas, he no longer had the time or the energy to make the most of the opportunity, so he decided to pass it on to someone who could.

The Professor devised a fiendishly puzzling conundrum and posted it in *The Times*, with a challenge for children everywhere to solve it.

The prize was his entire fortune.

The only condition was that the winner spent the money following the Professor's dream of travelling the world, and that they write back to him with stories of all the places they visited, the people they met and everything they experienced on their adventures.

Children everywhere sharpened their pencils and stepped up to the challenge. Most of them solved it without too much trouble and sent in their solutions.

One boy, named Arlo Banks, found the answer in no time. It had been easy. Far too easy, it seemed, to merit an entire fortune. So, he kept puzzling until another answer revealed itself. This had been the answer the Professor was looking for, and so it turned out that Arlo was the child he was looking for.

After a few weeks of frantic packing and phone calls, Arlo arrived at Victoria station carrying his suitcase and a ticket for the Orient Express. A gaggle of reporters were there too, snapping photos of the famous puzzle-solver as he waved goodbye to his family and set off on his adventures.

Arlo found his cabin on board the train. Waiting there was a small brown leather satchel with a note from the Professor . . .

Dear Arlo,

I'm sorry I couldn't be there to see you off; my health has taken an unfortunate turn.

I wish you well on your travels, but be warned: you are about to enter a world of mystery and murder. Clues will be everywhere. It's your job to find them, follow them and uncover the truths others wish to keep secret.

This may come as a surprise to you, but the world is a dangerous place. All kinds of enemies lurk in the shadows, even killers. Unmask them if you can. Beat them at their own games. Expose who they are, the reasons why they're doing these things and reveal how they commit their terrible crimes. They must be stopped.

This won't be easy, which is why I have left a gift for you. The satchel has served me well and I have added a few things that may prove helpful to make a detective's kit, of sorts. Keep it with you at all times.

Things are always more complicated than they seem, so you must remember this golden rule: Always avoid the obvious.

Yours sincerely,

Professor Hamatum-Sizzle

ARLO'S DETECTIVE'S KIT

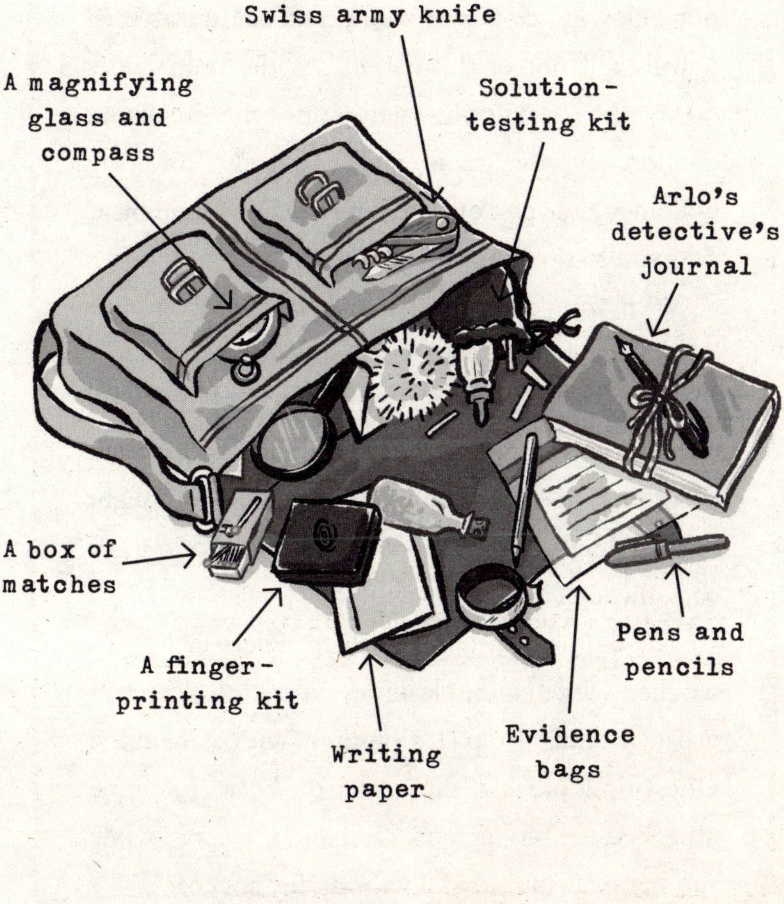

1

THE DINING CAR

With a loud blast of the whistle, the train sets off. Deep, puffing breaths rise from the funnel, blowing out billowing clouds of steam, and the train's steel wheels roll out of the station. As the train rattles down the tracks, you settle into the luxurious comfort of your cabin and watch the towering buildings glide past outside until the train announcer calls you to the dining car for breakfast.

With your detective's satchel hanging over your shoulder, you make your way along the train's narrow passageways. From the lace curtains framing every window, to the brass lamps that light the carriages, every inch of it feels as grand as a palace. You might be travelling the world, but this feels like a journey back through time.

The dining car is just as elegant. Every table has a starched white cloth, gleaming silver cutlery and an ornate reading lamp. It's bustling with passengers. One lady looks like she's been on board for some time because she arrives carrying a teapot, while another man appears still wearing his raincoat.

You're greeted by a smiling waiter, who checks you off the passenger list. 'This way, please,' he says, and shows you to an empty seat at one of the tables. Another boy is sitting opposite. He looks about two years younger than you.

'Hello, I'm Arlo Banks,' you say, sitting down.

The boy smiles. 'I'm Jamie Madden. I'm nine.'

'Keep it down,' barks a stern voice from across the carriage.

You look round to see the owner is a barrel-chested, red-faced man. You can't help wondering, *How can anyone be this angry so early in the morning, and in a wonderful place like this . . .?*

As you start reading the menu, Jamie leans over and whispers, 'Ignore my uncle. He's really stressed.'

Your eyes study Jamie and you can see a family resemblance. 'Why's he stressed? We're only ordering breakfast.'

Jamie laughs. 'It's not that. He's the chief of police. He's about to close a really big case.'

'Oh really?' you ask, immediately intrigued.

'He's got Luigi Cabrini locked in one of the cabins. He's quite old, but he's a big-time mafia godfather. We're transporting him for trial in Milan.'

You can't help shaking your head in disbelief. 'The *mafia?* They're seriously organized criminals,' you say.

'Yeah, it's true,' Jamie says. 'The whole train is full of Italian police in case he, or a member of his gang, tries anything.' As you look around the dining car, you realize that most of the people here are either in uniform or look like plain-clothes detectives. Jamie points to the man sitting behind you and says, 'That's Inspector Funaro. My uncle brought him along for his protection because he thinks someone is trying to kill him!'

'Really?' you ask as a sudden wave of nervousness courses through you. 'Why would anyone want to do that?'

Jamie whispers under his hand, 'So they can help Luigi Cabrini escape trial and spending the rest of his days in jail.'

This sounds like an extremely tall story, but Jamie is so convinced you can only believe it.

Chief Madden interrupts your thoughts with a snap of his fingers to get the smiling waiter's attention. 'Get me a Full English,' he demands. 'I can't start the day without one.'

The waiter nods and makes a note of it, then turns to take your order.

If you order:

- **Tea and Toast**, turn to **chapter 3**
- **Alpine Porridge**, turn to **chapter 5**
- **A Full English Breakfast**, turn to **chapter 2**

2

THE FULL ENGLISH BREAKFAST

Your order is the same as Chief Madden's, but after an unfortunate mix-up in the kitchen, you receive his Full English Breakfast.

A Full English Breakfast that's been poisoned.

You don't suspect a thing as you dip a slice of sausage into the perfectly runny yolk of your fried egg, then pop it into your mouth. You smile at Jamie as you chew, wondering how many more tall stories he'll tell you while the scenery glides past outside.

But you don't get to see the towering buildings merge into the countryside, or the fields rise into mountains, and Jamie doesn't tell you any more stories.

You don't even get to finish your breakfast before you collapse at the table.

Chief Madden was right to think someone was trying to kill him. But, this time, they killed you instead . . .

The Professor warned you for good reason. On this journey, dangers are lurking everywhere. But all is not lost! Try ordering something else and starting again. And if you sharpen your powers of deduction and avoid the obvious, you might just catch a murderer.

Good luck!

If you'd like to order:

- **Tea and Toast**, turn to **chapter 3**
- **Alpine Porridge**, turn to **chapter 5**

3

TEA AND TOAST

Within a couple of minutes, the smiling waiter returns and places a plate of perfectly browned toast and a steaming pot of tea on the table in front of you. You can't help smiling at the selection of jams laid out in little cut-glass dishes.

Chief Madden's Full English Breakfast arrives too, and it's huge. There are sausages, bacon, eggs, mushrooms, beans and a pile of toast. The Chief smothers it all in brown sauce and tucks in.

Before the butter has melted into your toast, Chief Madden collapses face down into his breakfast. His head lands with a *THUD!* Cutlery and china cups clatter, spilling tea everywhere.

You immediately get up to help, thinking he might be choking. But it's too late. The poison works fast, and he's dead before you can check his pulse.

The true horror of the Chief's death hits you with the scent of bitter almonds. It's so strong it cuts through the aroma coming off the grilled sausages and bacon, and it makes you recoil.

A sudden thought strikes you: *Was Jamie right?* If he was, it means someone has set in motion a plan to free a dangerous mafia godfather, so there isn't a moment to lose!

Inspector Funaro and his officers jump up in alarm and start ordering everyone not to move. You notice that the spilled tea is rushing towards a letter lying on the table beside the Chief's breakfast. Your instincts tell you it could be important, so you quickly grab it to stop it from getting ruined.

Before you can open it, the waiter calls out, 'Quick! That man in the raincoat – he's running away!'

If you:

- **Chase the man in the raincoat**, turn to **chapter 8**
- **Stay and read the letter**, turn to **chapter 18**

4

THE CORI CAMBRIAN CONUNDRUM OF CABIN NO. 4

The passenger list tells you that someone called Cori Cambrian is staying in Cabin No. 4, so you run to the sleeping car before they can carry out the next step of their plan . . .

The wooden doorframe splinters as you force your way into the cabin.

To your surprise, the place is empty.

The only thing that tells you someone has been here is a duffel bag sitting on the bed. Presumably it's ready and waiting for the killer to grab before they make their getaway – along with the aged mafia godfather, Luigi Cabrini.

You open the bag. Instead of finding clothes, money and passports, along with everything else they'll need for a few weeks on the run, you find a bomb.

The timer says you have less than a minute to

figure out which wire to cut if you want to defuse it. As you weigh up your options, it also occurs to you that anyone who plants a bomb on a train full of police officers would know there's a chance it could be found.

So you can be sure that one of the wires is a decoy.

Chop-chop, precious seconds are slipping away and you need to cut the wire that completes the circuit to defuse it. But be careful, snipping the decoy wire could set the whole thing off . . .

If you:

- **Cut the stripy wire**, turn to **chapter 38**
- **Cut the black wire**, turn to **chapter 27**
- **Run out of the cabin**, turn to **chapter 22**

5

THE ALPINE PORRIDGE

Chief Madden glowers as the smiling waiter hurries to the kitchen with the orders. 'If you burn my toast, I'll nick you for arson!'

Jamie rolls his eyes. 'I can't imagine why anyone would want to kill him, can you?'

You laugh. 'That's not really true, is it?'

'Yeah!' Jamie says. 'You can't arrest a major gangster and not get a few death threats. It goes with the job.'

Your intrigue goes into overdrive. But before you can ask any more questions, the waiter returns with Chief Madden's breakfast. It's so big it can barely fit on the plate. There are sausages, bacon, eggs, mushrooms, beans and a pile of toast. He smothers it in brown sauce and tucks in.

Before the waiter returns with your porridge, Chief Madden collapses face down with a *THUD!* Cutlery and china cups clatter, spilling tea everywhere.

You immediately get up to help, in case he's choking. But it's too late. The poison works fast, and he's dead before you can check his pulse.

The horror of the Chief's death hits you with the scent of bitter almonds. It's so strong it cuts through the aroma coming from the pile of grilled sausages and bacon on the Chief's plate.

As the smell makes you recoil, you notice something lying beside the Chief's breakfast. It's a letter! Something about it tells you it's important, so you pick it up.

Before you can open it, a sudden thought strikes you: *Was Jamie right?* If he was, it means someone has set in motion a plan to free a dangerous mafia godfather, so there isn't a moment to lose!

As alarm bells ring in your head, the waiter calls out, 'Quick! That man in the raincoat – he's running away!'

If you:

- **Chase the man in the raincoat**, turn to **chapter 8**
- **Stay and read the letter**, turn to **chapter 18**

6

CLIMBING ON TO THE ROOF

The window catch opens easily, as though it's been opened recently. The rushing noise of the wind fills the cabin as the train streams through the alpine valley. You feel its icy chill and it chaps your face.

As the train clatters along the tracks, you bravely climb out on to the window ledge and reach up to grip the trim that runs along the edge of the carriage roof.

You pull your body up and your feet leave the squidgy comfort of the bed's soft mattress.

The wind whips around you as the steam engine lets out a shrill *PEEP!* The sound is designed to startle everything from birds to trespassers on the line, and you can't help flinching. But you hang on tight and climb on to the roof.

Looking around, you discover the roof of carriage No. 3 is a maze of lights, air vents and skylights that have been numbered and renumbered over the years by various maintenance crews. See if you can find a pattern in the numbers and use it to guide you along the carriage roof to a place where you can get down safely. Remember, you're on top of a moving train so you need to be careful – you don't want to hurry or else you might put a foot wrong . . .

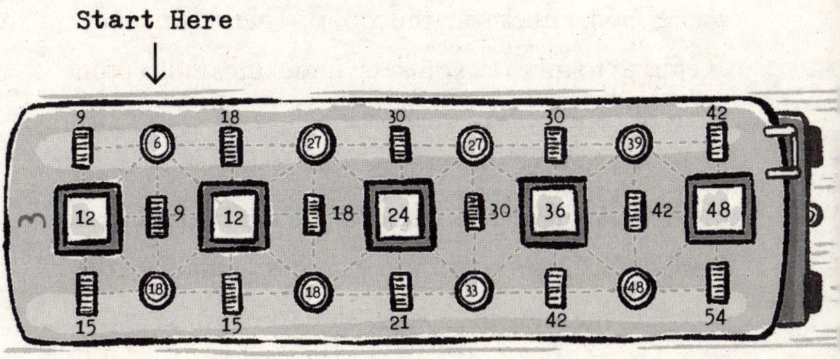

If you arrived at:

- **Air vent 42**, turn to **chapter 32**
- **Skylight 48**, turn to **chapter 28**
- **Air vent 54**, turn to **chapter 10**

7

RIC RAMI BACON'S CABIN NO. 7

You race to Cabin No. 7, certain you have the right name, and knock on the door. There's no reply. Refusing to give up, you keep knocking until a train steward comes along the corridor.

'Can I help at all?' he asks.

'Yes. I'm trying to find the person booked into Cabin No. 7,' you reply. You glance up and down the carriage, checking the coast is clear, then whisper, 'It's in connection with the murder that just happened.'

The moment you mention 'murder', the steward pulls a set of keys from his pocket. 'Happy to help an investigation,' he says as he finds the master key to the cabins and opens the door of No. 7.

To your surprise, the cabin is completely empty. The bedding is untouched. Even the complimentary chocolates haven't been eaten!

'This is odd,' you say.

'No it isn't,' the steward replies. 'This passenger must've missed the train. Happens all the time.'

Your certainty drains away as you take another look around the cabin and it becomes clear that Ric Rami Bacon was the wrong name.

Disappointed, you return to the dining car and tell the police your anagram theory about Ric Rami Bacon came to nothing. The officers listen politely but as soon as you finish, they all start laughing at you – the young boy who won a puzzle competition and thinks he's smart enough to solve a murder! Within the next two minutes they've found another five anagrams within the names on the list, and a couple are so rude, they're unrepeatable.

Laughter echoes around the carriage as they read them out. As your cheeks burn with embarrassment, Inspector Funaro ruffles your hair and says, 'In future, young man, leave this kind of thing to the professionals.'

It hurts. You've come so far, but this is the end of the line.

Jamie offers you a kind smile. 'Thanks for trying,' he says. 'You did your best.'

THE END

8

THE LOCKED DOOR

You race after the suspect, weaving through the carriages as the train rattles along the tracks. Police officers and passengers are coming out of their cabins to see what the commotion is all about. You push past and a few shout angry words after you.

Ahead of you, the man in the raincoat shoves past an elderly couple, leaving them stunned. As you rush by, the lady tuts loudly and the gentleman exclaims, 'Well I'll be!'

You don't stop to apologize and keep your sights on the man in the raincoat.

You run through the lounge car, hurrying past tables and comfy seats. As the suspect passes the bar, you call out, 'STOP THAT MAN!' But the bartender lets him go, shrugging as he polishes a glass.

The man in the raincoat reaches the sleeping car, where the narrow corridor bends, and he ducks out of sight. You follow him and discover that the carriage is lined with cabin doors.

You quicken your pace, but the suspect gets away from you. As he reaches the next carriage, he turns and shuts the adjoining door between you.

The wheels of the train clack and clatter along the steel tracks.

As you reach the door, there's no mistaking the click as the suspect locks it.

You hammer your fists against the window, but all the man does is smile. It's a leering, bully's smile, filled with satisfaction.

Little does he realize that your detective's kit contains a journal with a section on how to pick locks. You peer into the keyhole and immediately recognize it as a five-pin tumbler lock. You flick through the journal until you find a diagram that shows you how these locks work.

Five-pin tumbler lock

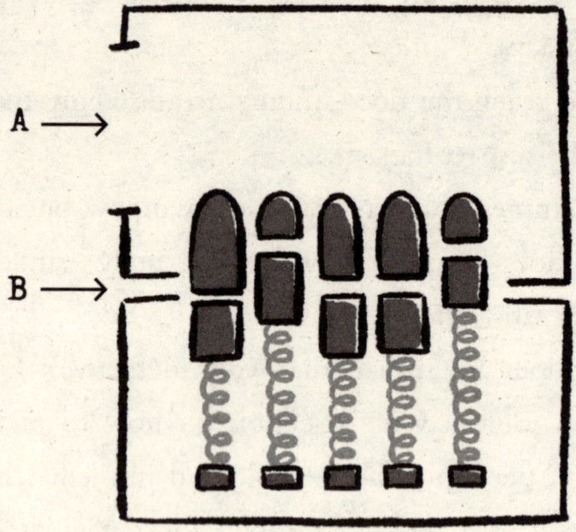

The key is inserted into the lock at Point A. The internal mechanism relies on the key pushing down each of the five sprung pins into their correct positions. When the spaces in the pins align with the barrel (Point B), the lock will open.

Your hands dive into your pockets and fish out a paperclip, the staple that held your train tickets together and a pin badge. See if you can put them together to make a lock pick that'll push down the pins in the right order so they align and open the lock. You might not need to use all of the items.

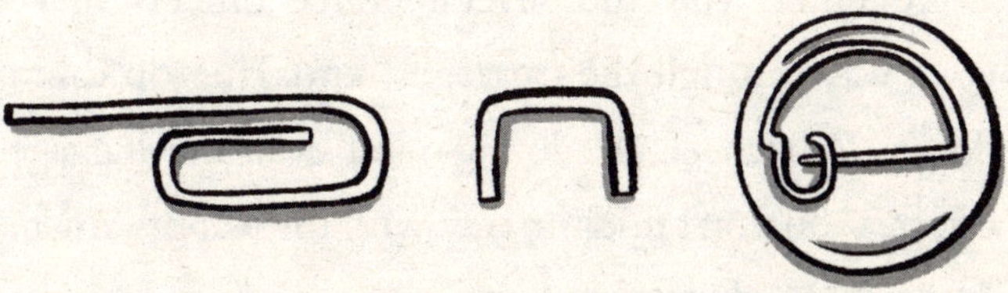

If you make a lock pick out of:

- **The pin badge and the paperclip**, turn to **chapter 39**
- **The paperclip and the staple**, turn to **chapter 23**
- **All three things**, turn to **chapter 43**

9

THE LADY WITH THE TEAPOT

'It's the lady with the teapot,' you say. You seem so convinced, Inspector Funaro orders a thorough search of the train and invites you to help.

Together, you and several police officers make your way through the carriages, knocking on cabin doors. You check the lounge and even the luggage car, but you don't find the lady with the teapot. You're so busy searching the train, none of you notice a member of the Cabrini mafia family emerging from their cabin as the train approaches the Mont Cenis Tunnel, which cuts through thirteen-and-a-half miles of the French Alps.

As you enter the tunnel, the train plunges into darkness, and that's the last thing you see.

The train and everyone on board never leave the tunnel. To this day, the murder of Chief Madden remains unsolved because there's nothing to go on. All the evidence, potential witnesses, bodies, even Luigi Cabrini and the entire train, mysteriously vanish.

Over the next few decades dozens of books and countless newspaper articles are written, filled with rumours, conjecture and speculation about the intriguing tale of what happened on your trip aboard the Orient Express. But the only thing anyone knows for sure is: none of you were ever seen again.

THE END

10

AIR VENT 54

The speed of the train and the rushing wind are disorientating. You reach the end of the train and have no idea how you ended up on this side of the carriage.

As you start trying to figure out how to get down off the roof, you spot a metal maintenance ladder on the other side of the carriage doorway that would get you safely down to the footplate between the carriages.

But there isn't time to turn back so you jump down. In your haste, you mistime your landing and fall past the footplate. The last thing you see is the rushing blur of gravel and sleepers as you fall from the train and land on the tracks.

Sadly, your life is lost, along with all the evidence you found.

Chief Madden's murder is never solved, Marco Cabrini escapes and Luigi Cabrini returns to the criminal underworld. Even though the police keep the case open, neither of the gangsters ever answer for their crimes.

THE END

11

ONE LAST RIDDLE

The door of Cabin No. 11 is unlocked. You duck inside, intending to start searching for clues to Chief Madden's murder.

Instead, you find a young man sitting by the window.

He's wrapped in layers of thick woolly jumpers and blankets to keep his gaunt body warm. His skin has an acidic yellow tint and the bottom half of his face is covered with a cotton mask.

'Come in,' he says with a wheezing breath and pulls down the mask to reveal a malevolent smile.

You have more pressing things to do but the look in his cloudy eye keeps you rooted to the spot. 'I . . . I have to get going,' you say, searching for an excuse to get out of there. But your words escape you as he pulls a gun from inside his cardigan. The door closes behind you.

'Please, Arlo. I am asking nicely,' he says, and points the gun at you.

Your eyes narrow into a frown. 'How do you know who I am?'

'Everyone knows Arlo Banks, the famous puzzle-solver,' he replies. 'As soon as I saw you on the platform, waving as the reporters snapped their photos, I hoped our paths would cross.'

'Really?' you ask. 'Why?'

'I think you can help me,' he says.

You look down at the gun. It seems unnecessary to hold someone at gunpoint when you're asking for their help, but you aren't in a position to argue.

'What do you want?' you ask.

The man's smile vanishes and he cocks the gun. 'That would be telling. But I will say this: your famous puzzling skills could give me a new lease of life.'

Your instincts tell you to run, but he's got you cornered.

'OK,' you say, putting your hands up. 'Let's have it.'

His smile returns and he gives you a riddle:

> I'm remembered, though I cannot remember why. What am I . . . ?

You ask if the answer is, 'Am I dead?'

'Yes, you are,' he replies, and the gun goes off!

THE END

12

MARCO CABRINI OF CABIN NO. 12

The cabin door is locked. You're so convinced this is the right place, you shove it with your shoulder. A wooden panel in the door snaps. With another couple of shoves, it gives way. You reach through the broken hole in the door and open the lock from the inside.

The air is cool and fresh but the window is closed, and the cabin is a mess as though Marco Cabrini left in a hurry. There's no sign of his raincoat. A suitcase has been emptied on the bed. Clothes, shoes and a wash bag have been strewn across the floor. Was Marco looking for the passport you found lying in the corridor?

Lying on the floor is something that catches your eye. It's a small brown medicine bottle. As your thoughts race, you open your satchel and take out your fingerprinting kit.

You dust the bottle with powder and find a

perfect fingerprint on the glass. Taking care not to smudge it, you place a piece of sticky tape over the print, then peel it off to make a record of it.

The bottle is full of a clear liquid. You twist open the lid and are instantly hit with a scent of bitter almonds. It's exactly the same smell you caught coming from the Chief's breakfast.

You quickly put the lid back on and preserve it in an evidence bag, then you take out your detective's journal and find the section on poisons.

There's a list of all kinds – arsenic, anthrax, even deadly nightshade – and how to spot signs of them. You soon discover that the scent of bitter almonds is an indicator of cyanide, one of the fastest and most deadly poisons there is.

It's not every day you realize you're holding a murder weapon, so you put the bottle safely in your satchel and turn your attention back to catching Marco Cabrini.

As you wonder where he might've gone, two theories pop into your mind, closely followed by a curious third possibility. So you write them down in your detective's journal:

1. Marco is a slippery customer. Did he somehow sneak past you and get to the carriage?
2. Mafia gangsters and murderers are capable of anything. But without his passport, Marco could've hit a dead end.
3. Besides the door, the only way out of the cabin is through the window. But you're in the Alps, miles away from the nearest station, why would he do something so risky?

You look around the messy cabin and start noting down a list of clues that might help you work out where Marco has disappeared to:

Clues

1. He either made the mess looking for his passport or did it to distract you while he made his escape into the carriage.
2. The only ways out of the cabin are through the door or the window.
3. If he hit a dead end, his only option would be to hide in the cabin.
4. The window only leads to the roof.
5. The bedding has been disturbed, but only the blanket is big enough to conceal a grown man.
6. If he climbed on to the roof, he must have another plan in mind.
7. If he's about to rescue Luigi, he would have gone to the carriage.
8. The air in the cabin is cool and fresh.

The last thing you do is draw a grid in your detective's journal. Now go back through the clues and your theories. Cross off the clues that contradict each other, tick the pieces of information that fit together, and use your conclusions to illuminate other details.

	CLIMBING THE ROOF	SNEAKS INTO THE CARRIAGE	HIDE IN THE CABIN	HE HAS HIT A DEAD END	HE IS RESCUING LUIGI	HE HAS ANOTHER PLAN
THE BLANKET						
THE MESS						
THE WINDOW						
HE HAS HIT A DEAD END						
HE IS RESCUING LUIGI						
HE HAS ANOTHER PLAN						

Now use your powers of deduction to draw your conclusions:

Marco used ______________________________

so he could ______________________________

because ______________________________

If you think Marco:

- **Sneaked past you to rescue Luigi**, turn to **chapter 37**
- **Climbed on to the roof**, turn to **chapter 6**
- **Is hiding under the bed**, turn to **chapter 46**

13

MARCUS HIGGINS OF CABIN NO. 13

You knock on the door of Cabin No. 13. A sign hanging on the handle says DO NOT DISTURB, but you try it anyway and find it's locked. The thought of a murderer getting away urges you not to give up.

You give the handle another turn and shove your shoulder against the door. The door flies open with the sound of splintering timber.

The back of the door collides with something soft and there's a dull *THUD!*

You stumble into the room to discover that you've knocked a police officer unconscious.

The sight of him lying on the floor takes you by surprise, but that's nothing compared to your shock at seeing a hulking great man stand up from a chair.

You shouldn't have ignored the DO NOT DISTURB sign!

His face is covered in battle scars. He has greasy, curly grey hair and looks old. His suit is struggling to hold in all his muscles, but his handcuffs rein him in. He smiles at you and says with a strong Italian accent, 'Guess there's been a change of plan.'

You gasp as words escape you.

'Well, come on then,' he says, and pushes past you.

It doesn't take you long to work out that the man locked in Cabin No. 13 isn't Marcus Higgins, it's Luigi Cabrini, the aged mafia godfather Jamie told you about. And you've just helped him escape!

THE END

THE TOILET

Congratulations! Your amazing powers of deduction and puzzle-solving have led you to . . . the toilet. It's small and cramped, filled with pristine porcelain and a neat little dish with a brass rail round the edge to protect the soap. Apart from a discrete air vent, the window is sealed so there's no way anyone could've escaped from here.

So, unless you need to use it, try another door . . .

Remember, there was a door slam just before you entered the sleeping car, and Marco won't have had any time to cover his tracks.

If you open:

- **Door 11**, turn to **chapter 11**
- **Door 12**, turn to **chapter 12**
- **Door 13**, turn to **chapter 13**

15

LOOSE END B

You pull the rope as hard as you can. At first it feels like the knot is resisting you, so you tug it again and again, until you realize you're just making it tighter.

You pick at the ropes, squeezing your fingertips in between the coils of binding fibres, but it's no use. You can't find any way to loosen them. In desperation, you try the other loose end, but you've tightened that too.

Gradually, as the sun begins to set, a train arrives further down the track to rescue Jamie and all the other passengers. But they don't rescue you.

Weeks later, after the crash site has been fully examined and the wrecked train has been removed, the line is reopened and you're found, so exhausted and weak from hunger and dehydration that it's too late to save you.

The police had worked on the assumption you'd been thrown from the train and were hoping to find you in a hospital somewhere. But as the reality comes to light, people all over the world mourn the loss of your puzzle-solving potential.

The only good news is, Marco Cabrini's passport and the bottle of poison you found link the mafia men to Chief Madden's murder *and* yours, making the police even more determined to catch him.

THE END

16

EXAMINE THE GUN

There's only one reason why a gun would be lying here: Marco must've dropped it.

You immediately open your satchel, take out your fingerprinting kit and start dusting. The powder reveals several small sections of fingerprints – two on the handle, one on the barrel and a thin strip of a fingerprint on the trigger.

If you can match any of the fingerprint sections to the print you found on the bottle of cyanide, you will have found an undeniable piece of evidence that connects the revolver Marco Cabrini fired at you with the murder weapon you found in his cabin. And together with the waiter's eyewitness account of Marco running from the scene in his raincoat shortly before Chief Madden's death, it will be enough to get him convicted in any court and sent to jail for a long time.

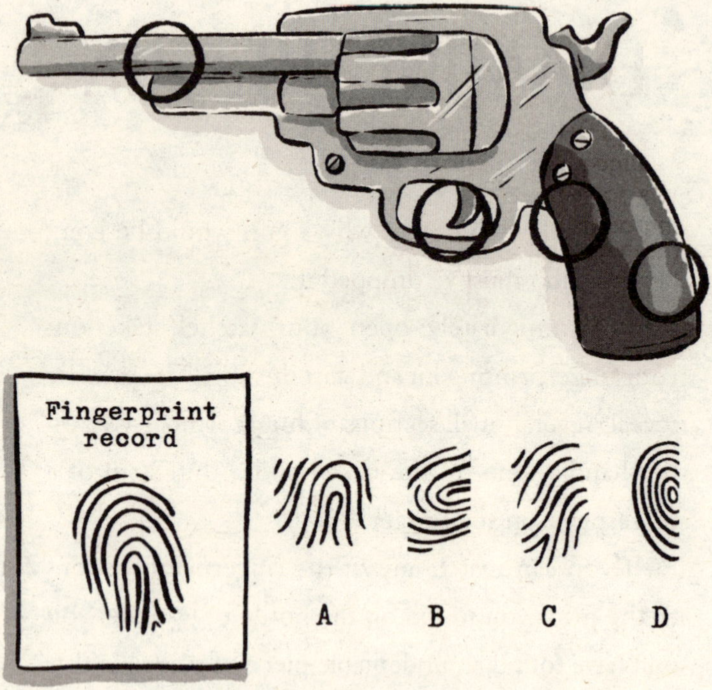

If you match the fingerprint record with:

- **Section A**, turn to **chapter 20**
- **Section B**, turn to **chapter 47**
- **Section C**, turn to **chapter 26**
- **Section D**, turn to **chapter 40**

17

THE GREY-HAIRED MAN

You conclude it was the grey-haired man. Inspector Funaro orders a search of the train and invites you to join the hunt for the suspect.

Eventually you and the Inspector reach the sleeping car, which is lined with doors to the cabins. You knock and an old man with grey hair opens the first cabin. He's surprised to see you, but his expression turns to alarm when the Inspector pulls out his police badge and introduces himself.

'We're investigating a murder and you were seen in the kitchen shortly before the victim died. Can you tell us what you were doing there?' he asks.

The man looks taken aback, and exclaims, 'A *murder*, you say?'

'Yes, that's correct,' the Inspector replies. 'Can you answer my question, please?'

'Well . . .' the old man stammers. 'I only went there to ask if we could order breakfast to be served in our cabin. My wife and I don't like crowds, you see.'

He opens the door to reveal his elderly wife sitting at a table by the window. Their breakfast is laid on a tray. Until you knocked on the door, they were enjoying tea and toast and watching the countryside go by.

Inspector Funaro nods. 'I see. Sorry to have interrupted you.'

He takes the man's name in case they need to ask him any questions in future, but you can both see that this is a dead end.

He turns to you. 'Thank you for your help, Arlo. We'll take it from here.'

You return to the dining car to write a very short and disappointing letter to the Professor.

THE END

18

THE LETTER

As horrified shock grips the carriage, you nervously open the envelope and pull out a folded piece of notepaper. The writing inside is printed, and its message is clear:

> Dear Chief Madden,
>
> We thought it was only polite to tell you that we're going to take care of you on the Orient Express. You can be sure of it.
>
> Ari Cabin Corm

You immediately spot that the name is not a real person, so it's most likely an anagram.

This makes it an important clue.

You grab the passenger list the smiling waiter

checked you off against, and set about working out if it's an anagram of someone on the train . . .

Passenger	Cabin No.
Mike Wilson-Stewart	15
Cori Cambrian	04
Ric Rami Bacon	07
Mable C. Dinki	21
Marcus Higgins	13
Marco Cabrini	12
Ms Callisonski	31
Jonathan C. Parker	19
Amanda Carpenter	36
Arlo Banks	10
Jamie Mortimer	29

If you found:

- **Ric Rami Bacon**, turn to **chapter 7**
- **Cori Cambrian**, turn to **chapter 4**
- **Marco Cabrini**, turn to **chapter 25**

19

LOOSE END A

You pull the loose end and to your relief, the ball of knotted rope unravels. You pick yourself up and look back along the track. By the time you get to the train and tell the police that Marco and Luigi Cabrini are getting away, they'll be long gone. So you decide to follow the tracks and see where they went.

Eventually the track takes another turn, leading you into a secluded section surrounded by dense pine trees. The ground is covered in a carpet of dull brown needles. As you glance down at them, you spot something unmistakable lying on one of the sleepers: it's the revolver Marco fired at you.

If you decide to:

- **Pick up the gun**, turn to **chapter 33**
- **Examine the gun**, turn to **chapter 16**

20

FINGERPRINT SECTION A

As soon as you've finished dusting the gun, you pick it up and return to the site of the train wreck.

The police officers are taking care of the shaken passengers, while the senior detectives take notes from the scene.

Jamie is the first to see you approach and he runs over. 'We were so worried about you,' he says, but stops short as he spots the revolver in your hand. His jaw falls open in disbelief.

'It's all right,' you assure him.

But as you hold up the gun, Inspector Funaro orders you to, 'Hold it right there!'

You immediately put your hands up. Unfortunately, one is holding Marco Cabrini's revolver and the other is holding the bottle of cyanide that killed Chief Madden.

You protest your innocence as the officers disarm you, but they're only interested in wrapping up their investigation so they look as professional as possible.

Months later you appear in court, charged with the Chief's murder. You tell them the truth about everything you did. It was you who tried to stop the train, who found Marco Cabrini's passport, the poison and the gun with his fingerprints.

The police try to twist your words into a confession, but the evidence against you is flimsy and you never had a reason to kill Chief Madden.

The judge eventually throws out the case, so the whole investigation ends in a train wreck, just like your journey.

THE END

21

MABLE C. DINKI OF CABIN NO. 21

You knock on the door of Cabin No. 21. There's no sound at first, so you look up and down the carriage to check you're in the right place. There's no mistaking it – this is the only Cabin No. 21 on the train, so you knock again.

BANG! BANG! BANG!

The sound of padding feet echoes from inside and a voice shouts, 'What's all that racket?'

'Er, hello, can you open the door, please?' you ask.

There's a click and the door slowly opens. An elderly lady peers through the gap. 'What do you want?' she demands with a vicious scowl.

As you stare at her you realize there's no way this woman could've run the length of the train – she can barely walk the length of her cabin! Her face doesn't match the photo in the passport either, and she looks as confused as you are.

'I'm sorry,' you say. 'I think I must've made a mistake.'

The lady mutters something under her breath and shuts the door, leaving you to check the passenger list again to see if you can find the cabin Marco Cabrini is registered to, and possibly hiding in.

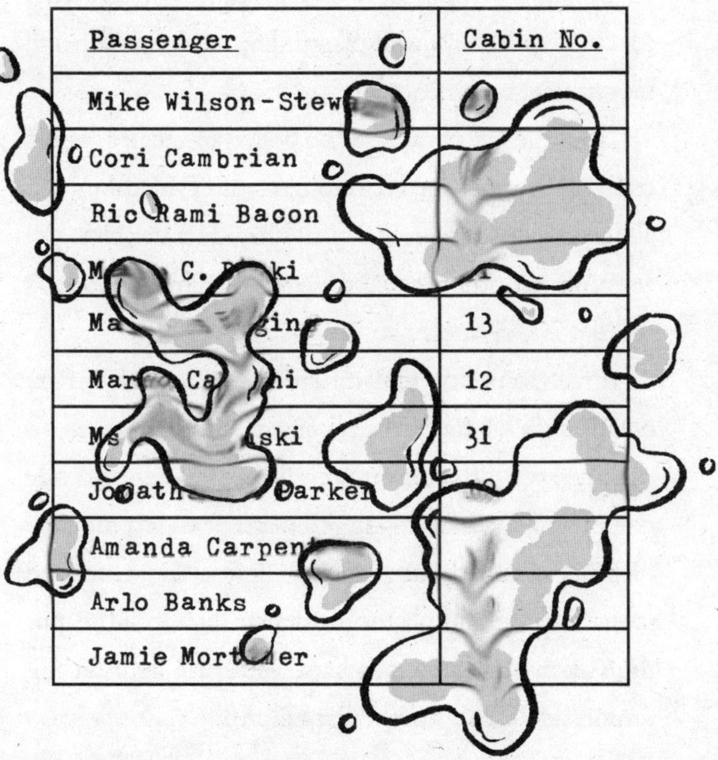

Passenger	Cabin No.
Mike Wilson-Stew	
Cori Cambrian	
Ric Rami Bacon	
M C. ki	
Ma gin	13
Mar Ca hi	12
Ms ski	31
Jo ath arke	
Amanda Carpen	
Arlo Banks	
Jamie Mort er	

Turn to the chapter of the cabin number you think he's hiding in.

22

RUN!

You get out of there and save yourself, just as the cabin explodes behind you. The entire train screeches to a halt with the squeal of grinding steel, but you and everyone else on board are safe.

Over the next few days the police and their forensic team sift through the charred remains of the cabin, but all the evidence inside it was destroyed by the blast.

With no other leads, the case of Chief Madden's murder is sadly never solved.

Jamie, Inspector Funaro and the other officers on board are all bitterly disappointed. To them, there is nothing worse than an unsolved murder, and this one comes with the added sting of a mafia boss escaping trial.

Since you had the chance to defuse the bomb and save the train and all the evidence that could've put the Chief's killer behind bars, you can't help feeling responsible for this particular failure.

You spend the rest of your days travelling the world, all the while wishing you could go back and defuse the bomb.

THE END

23

THE DROPPED CLUE

With one twist of your makeshift lock pick the lock clicks and the door swings open. You don't waste time congratulating yourself – there's a murderer on the loose and only you can catch them.

You run along past the cabins in the next sleeping car, but there's no sign of the man in the raincoat. You're about to double back to the dining car when you spot something lying on the floor.

It's a passport.

It could be anyone's. But there's a chance it was dropped by the man in the raincoat. You open it and find the photo inside matches the man who locked the door on you – you'd spot that bully's smile anywhere – and his name is: Marco Cabrini.

The surname instantly strikes a chord in your head.

If there's another member of the Cabrini family on the train, it can only mean one thing: they're here to help the mafia boss Luigi Cabrini escape!

The Cabrinis' plan is already in action so you must think fast . . .

The passport will easily persuade the police to question Marco Cabrini. But running from the scene and dropping it in the corridor aren't enough to connect him to the Chief's murder.

You slip the passport in an evidence bag for safekeeping but, as you put it in your satchel, a folded piece of paper brushes your hand. It's the letter you found when Chief Madden collapsed. You take it out and read it.

The writing inside is printed, and the message is clear:

Dear Chief Madden,

We thought it was only polite to tell you that we're going to take care of you on the Orient Express. You can be sure of it.

Ari Cabin Corm

You quickly realize that the letters of the name 'Ari Cabin Corm' are an anagram of Marco Cabrini, and you race back to the dining car.

Jamie is still sitting at your breakfast table, shaking his head in disbelief. 'I never thought someone would actually kill him,' he says as one of the police officers drapes a tablecloth over his uncle's body.

'I'm so sorry,' you say, looking around. Inspector Funaro is busy with his officers as they note down the details of the crime scene.

If they want to catch the killer, there isn't a moment to lose.

You go the table where the smiling waiter greeted you and grab the passenger list he checked your name against. It shows exactly who's on board and which cabin they're staying in.

Unfortunately, in the chaos that followed Chief Madden's murder, a jug of water spilled on the list, blurring the ink of the names. But there's still enough information for you to figure out which cabin Marco Cabrini is registered to, and possibly hiding in.

➡

Passenger	Cabin No.
Mike Wilson-Stew	
Cori Cambrian	
Ric Rami Bacon	
M C. ki	[illegible]
Ma ging	13
Mar Ca hi	12
Ms ski	31
Jonath Parker	[illegible]
Amanda Carpen	
Arlo Banks	
Jamie Mort er	

Turn to the chapter of the cabin number you think he's hiding in.

FOOTPRINTS SUSPECT C

You follow the footprints along the track as they meander through the valley. It would be a nice walk if you weren't on the trail of a murderer.

You quicken your pace, refusing to let Marco Cabrini get away. As you turn a corner, something up ahead makes you stop and stare.

Two men are a short distance in front of you.

One of them is wearing a long raincoat, and you immediately recognize him as Marco Cabrini. The other man is taller and wider, all heavy muscle, and even looks like someone from a gangster movie. He must be Luigi Cabrini, the aged mafia godfather Jamie told you was on the train. Chief Madden was right: their whole plan was designed to derail the train and wreck the case against Luigi, so he could get clean away!

It was perfect – they just didn't plan on you being here!

As much as you want to catch Chief Madden's

murderer, you're powerless to arrest or stop these two hardened criminals.

You decide to run back to the train and get the police. But before you can get away, a gunshot is fired into the air. The sound rings through the valley and you stop where you are.

Luigi Cabrini laughs as he strides along the track. 'I never thought I'd get caught by a kid,' he says with a rough chuckle. 'But I guess today's the day I caught *you*.'

Marco holds you at gunpoint while Luigi ties you to the railway tracks. 'See if you can figure your way out of that, *wise guy*!' Luigi says, tightening the last knot, and the pair of them walk off down the tracks.

As soon as they're gone, a wave of panic engulfs you. You listen out . . . The forest is peaceful and there's no sound of any approaching trains, so there's still a chance you can get out of this!

You stare down and closely examine the knots. Soon you realize there could be a way out of this, you just need to work out which loose end will get them undone.

If you pull:

- **Loose end A**, turn to **chapter 19**
- **Loose end B**, turn to **chapter 15**

25

MARCO CABRINI

The moment you spot the name 'Marco Cabrini' you feel a rush of exitement. 'This is our suspect,' you tell Jamie, confidently pointing to the name on the passenger list.

His eyes widen, astounded. 'How is there another Cabrini on the train?'

Inspector Funaro's ears prick up and he comes over. You explain the logic of the anagram from the name on the threatening letter and show him the passenger list.

It also includes an anagram of the mafia godfather's surname. The Inspector can't doubt your logic, and shoots a scowl across the carriage at his officers. 'Why did none of you think to check the passenger list?' he demands.

They all look away, sheepish and embarrassed.

The Inspector shakes his head. 'This is good police work,' he tells you.

'But why is Marco Cabrini on the train and using his real name?' Jamie asks.

'A lot of criminals make silly mistakes,' the

Inspector replies. 'But not the mafia, and definitely not the Cabrinis. This is personal for them. He's using his real name because they want us to know who they are and what they've done.'

'If there's another member of the Cabrini family on this train, it can only mean one thing: they're here to help Luigi Cabrini escape!' you say.

Jamie and the Inspector both start nodding.

'I'm willing to bet you're on to something,' the Inspector says. 'Let's work together and see what we can find out?'

As you nod in agreement, a police officer ushers the smiling waiter, the chef and a train steward into the dining car.

'They each saw someone in the kitchen who shouldn't have been there when the Chief's breakfast was being prepared,' the officer explains. 'Any one of them could've slipped the poison into his food. So the question is: Who did it?'

'A man with grey hair came in, just as I was frying the eggs,' says the chef. 'He started asking me all sorts of questions about whether he and his wife could have breakfast served in their cabin instead of the dining car.' The chef shakes her head. 'I was too busy to answer him, so I told him to speak to the waiter.'

'Could he have slipped something into the food while you were cooking?' asks the Inspector.

'I was busy watching the eggs on the stove. But it's possible he added something to everything on the plate,' the chef concedes.

'OK. Who did you see?' the Inspector asks the waiter.

'The man in a raincoat. I called out, "He's running away," but no one did anything,' he says. 'He was in such a rush, I didn't see his face.'

Inspector Funaro nods and makes a note of everything.

'There was also a lady with a teapot,' the steward says. 'I don't know where she came from, but she made a huge fuss because her tea was stewed.'

'That could've been a distraction,' Inspector Funaro says as he makes another note and starts mulling this over.

Go through the witnesses' statements and see if you can find any clues in the word search that reveal which suspect you should start looking for.

I	H	B	Q	J	T	D	E	R
T	E	A	X	S	L	H	M	A
I	K	F	P	O	T	G	J	I
S	A	H	Y	N	L	R	I	N
T	V	R	I	Y	W	E	H	C
H	T	N	G	W	R	Y	A	O
E	A	Y	A	H	F	C	I	A
M	D	U	X	I	Y	B	R	T

If you think it's:

- **The grey-haired man**, turn to **chapter 17**
- **The lady with the teapot**, turn to **chapter 9**
- **The man in the raincoat**, turn to **chapter 30**

FINGERPRINT SECTION C

Try as you might, you can't make any of the fingerprints from the gun line up with the print you took from the poison bottle. No matter how you turn them round, it's no good. You get so frustrated, you try to take the prints again, but you get so much powder on the gun, you spoil the prints, and in no time you realize your efforts have ruined the evidence.

Disappointment seeps into your bones and you give up. All that's left to do is take the gun and the poison bottle back to the train wreck and hope the police can figure something out . . .

Jamie and Inspector Funaro listen to your story. At first they're impressed that you took on the case and lived to tell the tale.

But the fingerprints were key pieces of evidence – vital for any case against the killer. And now you've ruined them, the case will most likely never result in

Marco or Luigi Cabrini being jailed for Chief Madden's murder.

You're very sorry, but Jamie is bitterly disappointed in you.

THE END

27

THE BLACK WIRE BANG!

As the timer runs down, you decide to cut the black wire.

Your cutters expose the wire's copper core, sending the timer into overdrive and the remaining seconds run away from you.

In that instant, you realize you've cut the wrong wire, but it's too late.

The bomb explodes, destroying the cabin and the entire sleeping car, along with you and everything else inside it.

Fire from the bomb sweeps through the train. Every shred of evidence that could have been used to catch the killer is incinerated.

Chief Madden's murder will never be solved now . . . and neither will yours.

THE END

SKYLIGHT 48

You stop at the end of the carriage. Standing on the skylight, you look around and wonder what to do next. There's a metal ladder leading down to the footplate, but it's too far to jump to.

You're suddenly very aware that you're standing on top of a train, speeding through the mountains. And you can't afford to put a foot wrong.

On second thoughts, it might be a good idea to turn round and retrace your steps from the beginning. And this time, try not to put a foot wrong!

Return to **chapter 6**

29

WRONG NUMBER

You dial the number and it starts ringing, but no one answers. You try it again, but this time the call is cut off and the line goes dead.

It was worth a try, but the only conclusion you can draw from this is that the numbers on the phone aren't the only thing that's been vandalized. So you hang up and continue following the footprints . . .

Eventually the track leads you to a section of the line that's surrounded with pine trees. Their scent fills your nostrils. You glance down at the carpet of brown pine needles and spot something unmistakable lying on the tracks: a loaded revolver.

If you:

- **Pick up the gun**, turn to **chapter 33**
- **Examine the gun**, turn to **chapter 16**

30

THE MAN IN THE RAINCOAT

The moment the clues fall into place you feel certain the man in the raincoat knows something about Chief Madden's murder.

Inspector Funaro agrees and orders a search of the train. This is a police matter, but there's no time to lose, and since you've proved to be very helpful so far, Inspector Funaro invites you to join the search.

While the police start knocking on cabin doors, you head to the sleeping car. You figure that if the man in the raincoat is making his getaway, he won't be hanging around the crime scene, and the cabins would be an ideal place to hide.

You search the sleeping car but there's no sign of a man in a raincoat, or anyone else who could match his description. You're about to cut your losses and return to the dining car when you spot something lying on the floor.

It's a passport.

You open it and find it belongs to Marco Cabrini.

This can only mean one thing: The Cabrinis' plan to help Luigi escape is already in action, so you must think fast . . .

The passport will easily persuade the police to question Marco Cabrini. But the witness report of him running from the scene and dropping it in the corridor won't be enough to prove he's guilty of the Chief's murder.

You slip the passport in an evidence bag for safekeeping. As you put it in your satchel, you hear someone enter the far end of the carriage. You look up and see Marco Cabrini – and he's wearing a raincoat and must've come back to look for his passport.

Your eyes connect, then he turns and runs away.

You chase Marco Cabrini through the train, but he is too slippery and you lose sight of him. As you reach the last carriage in the train, you hear a door slam.

Marco must've gone into one of the four cabins, but he hasn't had time to cover his tracks.

See if you can spot the different clues and work out which door he went through.

But be careful. Searching cabins can waste a lot of time and even land you in a lot of trouble.

If you open:

- **Door 11**, turn to **chapter 11**
- **Door 12**, turn to **chapter 12**
- **Door 13**, turn to **chapter 13**
- **Door 14**, turn to **chapter 14**

31

MS CALLISONSKI OF CABIN NO. 31

As soon as you realize the name on the Chief's letter fits with the name of the passenger in Cabin No. 31, you rush to the sleeping car.

But to your surprise, the door is opened by an older woman who looks like a fairground fortune teller. 'There you are,' she says. 'I've been waiting for you. Come in.'

You're so taken aback by her welcoming and polite manner that you drop your guard and enter the cabin.

The cabin has a strange, slightly smoky aroma, but you can't see anything that's actually burning. 'Please,' says the lady, and she invites you to sit at a little fold-away table by the window.

'Were you in the dining car earlier?' you ask, keen to get down to business as the mountains flash past.

The lady puts a finger to her lips to shush you and pours some tea. 'All your questions will be answered soon enough,' she assures you.

You don't have time for this, but since it's the best lead you have, you've little choice but to go along with her game.

'All my life I've read tea leaves,' the lady explains. 'They speak to me; tell me things the rest of the world can't imagine.' She looks into your eyes. 'And they've served me well.'

'Don't you like the tea they serve on the train?'

The lady shakes her head. 'I only ever drink my own,' she says, and hands you a china cup with a quaint saucer. 'Here. Let's see what your leaves have to say.'

You blow the steam off your tea and drink it as quickly as you can, so as not to waste another second. The tea burns slightly as you swallow, but you try to ignore that.

The lady takes your cup and looks into it.

'I'm investigating a murder,' you say, to hurry her along.

'How is that possible?' the lady asks, raising an eyebrow. 'It hasn't happened yet.'

You try to explain, but the words won't come out. A wave of alarm crashes over you, but it's too late. Your vision blurs and you slump in your seat.

Sixteen months later, your body is found by a group of hikers. It appears you jumped from the train, but no one will ever uncover the truth of how you ended up there.

THE END

32

AIR VENT 42

As the train rattles along the tracks, you reach the end of the carriage and look down. Just below you is a metal ladder welded to the train that's used by the maintenance crew. The sight of it comes as a welcome relief, and you climb down.

You reach the safety of the steel footplate jutting out from the luggage car and look around to get your bearings. There's no door to let you back into the train carriage, so Marco Cabrini must've climbed up and over the coal tender to the steam engine.

It feels like the train is speeding up as you step on to the coal tender and climb up another maintenance ladder. You look across the mound of coal that's powering the train. The rushing wind is blowing dust off the edges of the dusty lumps, but you don't have time to worry about that now. You start scrambling across the coal towards the engine.

As the train thunders down the tracks, steam from the funnel rushes through your hair, blowing up clouds of coal dust around you. You press on until you reach the engine.

As you climb down into the engine, you realize why the train is going so fast. The driver and fireman are lying unconscious, having been knocked out by someone wielding a coal shovel. Pieces of pipework from the train's boiler are lying scattered around them.

See if you can put the pipes back in the correct places to reconnect the boiler. You need to work quickly. The train is careering out of control!

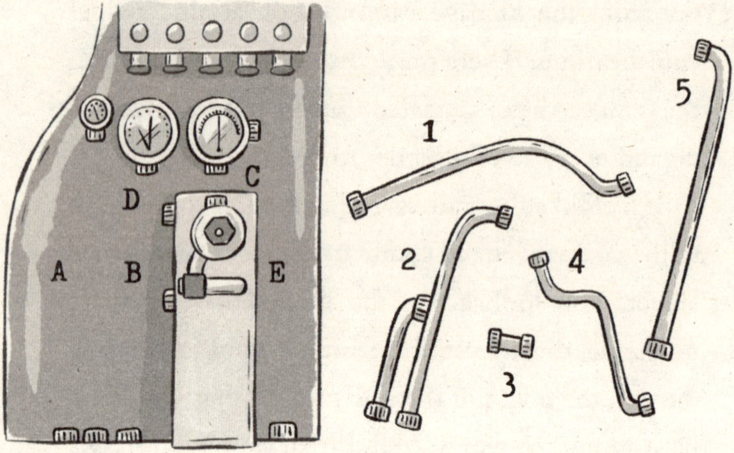

If:

- **All the pipes fit into place**, turn to **chapter 36**
- **The pipes won't fit**, turn to **chapter 34**

33

PICK UP THE GUN

From the moment you feel the weight of the gun in your hand, its power makes you feel strong enough to take on the whole world, so a mafia thug who's stupid enough to drop their weapon should be easy enough to apprehend.

You follow the footsteps along the tracks until they turn off down a path that leads into the woods.

Within a few minutes the smell of wood smoke overpowers the scent of the pine forest. A short walk away, you find it coming from the chimney of a secluded cabin.

A fresh footprint on the path confirms that this is where Marco Cabrini is hiding out. And you've got his gun.

You fire a bullet into the air and call out, 'Marco Cabrini. I know you're in there. Come out with your hands up. You're wanted for the murder of Chief Madden.'

Marco doesn't reply.

Instead, a couple of windows are smashed out and

he and Luigi Cabrini open fire with machine guns.

You dive behind the biggest tree and cower there as the gangsters unload their guns on you. As the bark and branches are shot to bits, the strength you felt holding the gun slips away, leaving you powerless and scared.

The noise of the gunfire cuts through the peaceful valley, all the way to the train wreck. The police hear the unmistakable sound and come as quickly as they can.

But by the time they arrive and find you huddled behind the shot-up tree, Luigi and Marco Cabrini are long gone and will never be caught.

THE END

DERAIL DISASTER!

No matter how hard you try, the pipes simply refuse to fit and reconnect to the boiler. If that's not frustrating enough, your time is running out!

The train's pistons pump in a furious blur, powering its wheels down the track. The towering mountains covered in fir trees flash past as the train careers through the valley towards a tight bend at the top of a steep embankment.

The sight fills you with horror.

But it's no good. Even if you reconnect the pipes now, there isn't enough track left for the train to stop.

You crouch down and brace for the impact of whatever's coming round the corner.

The train steams into the bend and careers off the track, as though the bend in the rails isn't even there. There's a moment's silence. You feel yourself lift off the footplate as the train hurtles through the air. It dives down a steep embankment at the foot of the mountain . . .

A moment later the reality of what's happening

hits home as the train crashes into the ground. Fir trees splinter, snapping like matches, as the huge steel steam engine thunders into the ground and starts rolling over and over and over, down and down the mountainside.

You're thrown around like a rag in a tumble dryer, until your head collides with the roof of the engine, and that's the last thing you remember.

THE END

35

EMERGENCY SERVICES

As you press the last digit, the phone line begins to murmur with a distant ringing.

A moment later your call is answered and a French person asks, 'Which emergency service do you require?'

'Hello,' you reply, as the French you studied comes back to you. 'There's been an accident. The Orient Express has derailed not far from here.'

'It's OK, stay calm,' the operator reassures you. 'We'll send a rescue team. Please return to the train and wait there. We're on our way.'

'Thank you,' you say. 'Please hurry.'

A few minutes later you return to the train. Jamie is talking to Inspector Funaro. As you approach, Jamie looks round and says, 'There you are! I was so worried. Where have you been?'

They both look relieved as you tell them the emergency services are on their way. Then you reveal all the evidence you've found that proves

Marco Cabrini murdered Chief Madden.

Inspector Funaro is very impressed and quickly gathers his officers to form a search party. 'Thank you, Arlo. You've done a brilliant job, but we'll take it from here,' he says, and they head off to track down and arrest Marco and Luigi Cabrini.

As they go, you feel a deepening sense of failure, that makes you wish you could go back and find a more satisfying outcome . . .

THE END

A SUDDEN STOP

The moment you put the last pipe in place, the boiler system breathes a sigh of relief and the dials and gauges come back to life. You feel a warm sense of success, too, but the train keeps racing down the tracks. You glance along the line and see a straight track cutting through the mountains towards a curve that veers round a steep embankment.

If you don't take evasive action, the train is going so fast it'll derail!

You stare at the dials and gauges as their needles pop and bounce, each one flicking one way then the other as the system struggles to stabilize itself.

You grab the only lever in front of you. It's known as the 'dead man's handle'. Usually it shuts off the boiler and stops the train the moment it's released, but Marco Cabrini jammed it into the ON position before he dismantled the pipes.

With all your strength, you try to pull it away from the ON position.

The train clatters down the tracks, towards the bend that should guide everyone on board safely between the mountains.

But it's no use. Marco hammered the metal into place to keep the train running. You grind your teeth and pull the lever as hard as you can, desperate to avoid a catastrophe.

As the train closes in on the bend, something gives and the handle shoots back. The train's brakes clamp down hard and the wheels let out an ear-splitting whine as they scrape along the steel tracks.

But it's too late to avoid a derailment!

The sudden stop throws you against the boiler dials. The pipes you reconnected dig into your chest and your head hits the pressure gauge.

The last thing you hear before blacking out is the sound of the dial's glass breaking as the train begins to tumble down the embankment . . .

Turn to **chapter 41**

37

RETURN TO THE CARRIAGE

You step over the mess and splintered doorframe back into the train carriage. Marco Cabrini is nowhere to be seen. It's unlikely he would return to the scene of the crime, with the police alerted and looking for him.

You run all the way to the other end of the train, but all you find is the locked cage at the entrance of the luggage car. It's padlocked from the outside and the inside is piled high with suitcases and wooden trunks.

It's like he's vanished into thin air – but he can't have.

You kick the cage in frustration, before running back to check his cabin again and look under his bed. All you find is an old sock left behind by another passenger.

There is no way anyone in the kind of rush Marco Cabrini was in would waste time covering their tracks this well. So your only conclusion is that you must've made a mistake somewhere, and this time it has let a killer get away.

THE END

38

THE STRIPY WIRE SMOKER

With a rush of certainty, you cut the stripy wire, but to your surprise the bomb explodes with a deafening *BANG!*

You cough and convulse as the cabin fills with smoke pouring from the detonator. To your relief, the explosives have remained intact.

That was a close one, but you've made it!

Still coughing and a little confused, you stumble into the corridor. A nearby door slams shut, and it feels like everything around you is moving too quickly. Your brain is trying to black out, but you refuse to let it. Each time you blink, you get a snapshot of the corridor.

You prop yourself up and shake the confusion from your head, then open a window and breathe in the refreshing mountain air as the train rattles along the tracks. It feels as good as a medicine.

As your senses return, you cast your mind back to the glimpses you saw of the corridor. Your senses tell you there could be something important – some tiny difference that could prove to be a clue.

Think hard and focus on these two mental images and see if you can spot an important difference.

When you think you've spotted a difference, see where it takes you.

If you've spotted:

- **A shadowy hand**, turn to **chapter 42**
- **Someone running away**, turn to **chapter 8**

If you spotted more than one difference, wrack your brain. Something in Marco's behaviour could give you a clue you can follow.

39

ONE LOCKED DOOR LEADS TO ANOTHER . . .

You twist and turn the lock pick, but it's no use – the door refuses to open.

The train hasn't stopped yet, so there's every chance you can still catch the man in the raincoat. You pull the lock pick out of the lock and decide to try again with a different combination of the items.

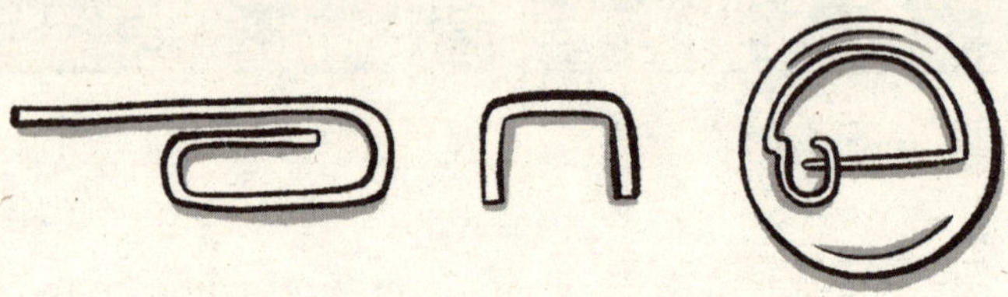

If you try:

- **The paperclip and the staple,** turn to **chapter 23**
- **All three things,** turn to **chapter 43**

FINGERPRINT SECTION D

As soon as you place fingerprint section D beside the print you found on the medicine bottle, you realize you've made an error. You've come so far and you're a better detective than a silly mistake like this.

You dismiss this fingerprint and look again at the other prints you found on the gun.

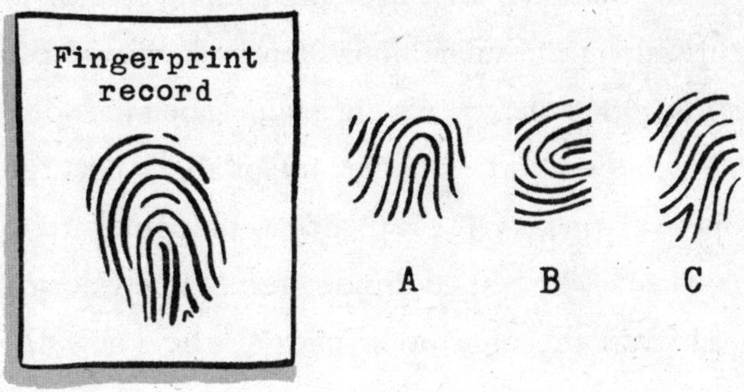

If you match the fingerprint record with:

- **Section A**, turn to **chapter 20**
- **Section B**, turn to **chapter 47**
- **Section C**, turn to **chapter 26**

FINDING FOOTPRINTS

You come to, covered in mud and pine needles. Your head is throbbing, but luckily all your bones are in one piece and where they're supposed to be. You pick yourself up and clamber out of the upturned steam engine.

The wrecked train is lying in a snaking column of debris along the valley floor. You look around and see the other shaken passengers are opening doors and windows and climbing out of the train. You hope everyone is OK . . . then your thoughts turn to the person who caused this disaster: Marco Cabrini.

He was the only other person who knew the crash was coming, so he must be here somewhere.

You look down at the ground and see trails of footprints in the mud churned by the train wreck. You jump down and start studying them. Most of the prints have been left by people helping the passengers off the train, but you feel certain that one set was left by Marco as he made his getaway.

If you've learned anything about Marco Cabrini, it's that he's quick and light on his feet. If you can work out which set was left behind by someone leaving the scene, there's still a chance you could catch a murderer . . .

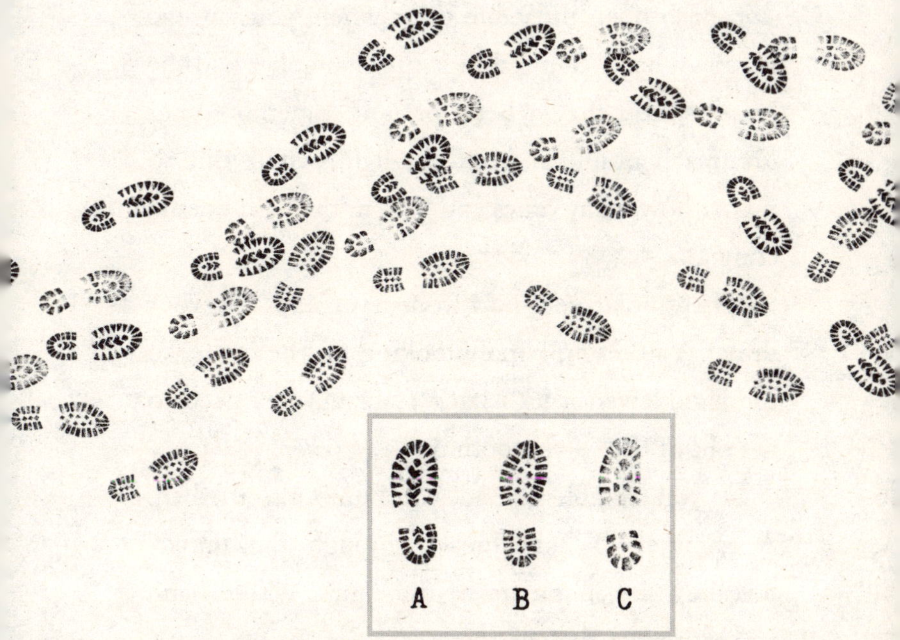

If you think Marco left:

- **Footprint A**, turn to **chapter 44**
- **Footprint B**, turn to **chapter 45**
- **Footprint C**, turn to **chapter 24**

THE SHADOWY HAND

You push open the cabin door where you saw the shadowy hand. The cabin is full of smoke. Did the bomb start a fire in here, or is it something else? You reach around and find the light switch. But no matter how many times you flick it, the light doesn't come on.

The smoke gets into your eyes and fills your throat. You reach, blindly looking for the owner of the hand. Even if it's Marco Cabrini, they need to get out of here – you both do!

As you stumble around, you bump into the bed. A glimmer of light breaks through the smoke, revealing the silhouette of the figure whose hand you spotted in the corridor.

You call out to them, but it's too late. Your head is spinning from the smothering smoke and you fall back on to the bed . . .

Down . . .

Down . . .

Down you sink into the soft mattress.

You blink as your eyes water, and you start to wince under the weight of a truly splitting headache. The silhouette steps forward, towering over you.

'I think I need an ambulance,' you murmur.

The silhouette shakes their head. 'No, my friend,' they reply. Their voice is slightly muffled by a face mask but you can still hear a strong Italian accent. 'You need a coroner.'

You reach out to them, pleading for their help, but they simply walk out of the cabin and leave you to die as they make their escape.

THE END

43

THE LOCKED DOOR

Despite your efforts, you can't pick the lock and get the door open. You hammer on the window in frustration, but the toughened safety glass refuses to budge.

You promise yourself that this doesn't mean the Chief's murderer has escaped, and return to the dining car.

You settle back into your seat opposite Jamie to watch the mountain scenery go by outside.

But it seems to be passing by so quickly, you can barely focus on anything – the trees, the rocks. Even the cabins on the opposite side of the valley begin to blur.

You put it down to the head-shrinker of a day you've had and close your eyes.

But you can't get to sleep before other people become concerned. Voices start calling out, 'The train, it can't stop.'

Outside, the trees and mountains flash past until . . .

The train reaches a curve and flies off the track.

Down the embankment you hurtle until the train ploughs into the mountainside. You don't stop there. The wreckage tumbles over and over, leaving a corridor of churned-up earth and broken trees. The disaster investigation team will spend weeks sifting through the wreckage.

It doesn't take them long to determine that this disaster was caused by someone who set out to derail the train, for reason or reasons unknown.

If you'd just managed to open the door, things could've turned out very differently.

THE END

FOOTPRINTS SUSPECT A

You follow the footprints up the steep embankment and along the train line. The peaceful stillness of the valley is only broken by the occasional tweet of birdsong and the wind when it rushes through the trees. This would be the perfect place for a picturesque hike, if you weren't tracking down a vicious murderer.

Eventually the footprints lead you to a railway siding where you find a telephone for emergencies. Anyone who was hurt when the train derailed will be needing medical attention, and the sooner it can get to them the better.

You decide to stop and call an ambulance. But as soon as you open the phone box, you find a vandal has rearranged and drawn all over the numbers and left you a message:

THEY SAY HOME IS WHERE THE HEART IS.
BUT FINDING LOVE WILL SAVE YOU!

A sign above the keypad tells you to contact the local emergency services on 112. If you can work out which buttons to press.

When you have a number to dial, choose an option below.

If you dial:

- **Eyeball, eyeball, heart,** turn to **chapter 35**
- **House, house, heart,** turn to **chapter 29**

45

FOOTPRINTS SUSPECT B

You follow the footprints further along the track, through twisting turns, heading deeper into the valley. Your legs grow tired but the fresh mountain air clears your head.

Eventually the track takes another turn, leading you into a secluded section of the line surrounded by pine trees. The ground is covered in a carpet of dull brown needles and their scent fills your nostrils.

As you glance down at them, you spot something unmistakable lying on the tracks: a loaded revolver.

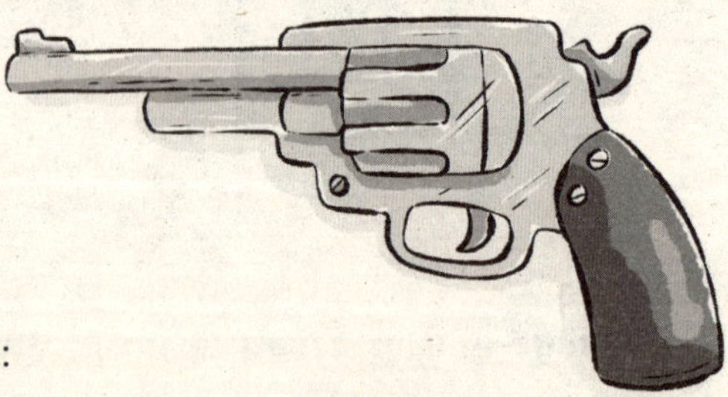

If you:

- **Pick it up**, turn to **chapter 33**
- **Leave it alone**, turn to **chapter 16**

UNDER THE BED

You freeze where you stand. Could Marco Cabrini really be hiding under the bed? If he is, he must've heard you breaking in through the door, looking through the things he left strewn around the cabin. It's possible he heard you find the bottle of poison he used to murder Chief Madden.

The only thing he doesn't know is that you're a young boy. He's probably expecting a fully grown, trained, maybe even armed police officer.

But if you go and get one, he will undoubtedly escape.

This is it: your big chance to catch a murderer!

You pull back the blanket with one yank. It flaps like a ship's sail in the wind. You expect Marco to be there, lying under the bed, but there's nothing here besides an old sock left behind by a previous occupant.

As you stare at the empty space, a wave of disappointment hits you. You were so sure he was hiding there.

But all is not lost. Not yet.

If you go back through the clues and work out where Marco Cabrini has disappeared to, you still have enough time to catch him.

Return to **chapter 12**

FINGERPRINT SECTION B

The section from the trigger lines up perfectly with the fingerprint from the poison bottle, and together they point the finger at Marco Cabrini. He poisoned Chief Madden and set the train to derail so he could help Luigi Cabrini escape the trial and avoid a lengthy spell in jail.

It's so clear now, it would be impossible for any judge and jury not to find them both guilty.

Examining the gun and dusting it for prints were the right thing to do, and so is handing all your evidence over to the police.

As soon as you've finished dusting the gun, you carefully pick it up to avoid damaging the fingerprints and slip it in an evidence bag, then return to the site of the train wreck. The police are helping take care of the rather shaken passengers. You approach Jamie and Inspector Funaro and tell them everything that's happened. The Inspector commends you on a job well done and orders his officers to form a search party.

'Can you take us to where you last saw them?' Inspector Funaro asks you.

'Sure,' you reply. 'It's just along the tracks.'

'Perfect,' he replies. 'Lead the way.'

A few minutes later you're back at the spot where you found the gun. You continue to follow the footprints along the tracks until they turn off and head into the forest. As you make your way through the trees, the smell of wood smoke filters through the scent of pine needles.

Inspector Funaro snaps his fingers and signals for everyone to stay quiet. You press on in silence until you come to a clearing with a small cabin. Wood smoke is coming from its chimney.

The police draw their guns and Inspector Funaro starts directing his officers to surround the cabin. As soon as every exit is covered, he marches up to the front door and hammers on it with his fist. 'Luigi Cabrini! It's the police. Come out with your hands up!'

Neither Marco nor Luigi reply. Instead, you're met with the sound of tinkling glass as they smash out a couple of windows and open fire with two machine guns.

Trees and branches are blasted apart as they unload their guns.

Your instincts tell you to duck as the police return fire. More windows smash and splinters fly as the wooden cabin is shot to bits, and the peaceful forest fills with the chaos of gunfire.

Eventually there's a pause in the noise as the Cabrinis reload, and Inspector Funaro calls out, 'Even if you survive this, you can't escape, Cabrini. We have the evidence to put you away for Chief Madden's murder.'

In one last act of defiance, Luigi and Marco Cabrini return fire. As soon as they're out of ammo, Inspector Funaro and his officers rush the cabin and arrest them both.

You watch from the trees as Luigi and Marco are brought out.

The mafia godfather might be old, but every bit of him is grizzled and tougher than an overcooked steak.

He looks at you and smirks. 'What's this, take your kid to work day?' he asks the Inspector.

'No, this is Arlo Banks,' Inspector Funaro explains.

'He's the detective who caught you.'

'Damn it, Marco!' Luigi exclaims.

'Sorry, Boss.' Marco shrugs. 'But that ain't no ordinary kid.'

The police lead them back to the train, where you all wait for the emergency services to arrive and take away the Cabrinis. Thanks to you, they will spend the rest of their lives in jail.

You ride a wave of elation that only comes from solving a case, all the way from the site of the train wreck to your hotel in Milan. You arrive, looking forward to a refreshing shower and enjoying some brainteasers by the pool. But before you can check in, the hotel manageress hands you a letter.

'It arrived about an hour ago, Mr Banks,' she explains.

'Thank you,' you reply. As soon as you realize it's from the Professor, all your thoughts of relaxing by the pool are replaced by the irresistible prospect of another adventure . . .

THE SCARAB'S REVENGE

Dear Arlo,

Congratulations on solving a truly puzzling murder!

You also succeeded in proving that my faith in you was indeed very well placed.

There has, however, been a slight change of plan. While you were puzzling your way through the mountains, the chance arose for you to join an exclusive cruise aboard the most luxurious ship on the Nile, and I thought it was too fantastically tantalizing for you to miss!

So, I bid you bon voyage. The waters of the Nile and the deserts of Egypt are beckoning, but you must be careful. It's a country full of ancient mysteries that have been lost in the sands of the desert and time. Many seasoned explorers have ventured there – some have come home cursed; others have never been seen again.

For your own safety, I implore you to make notes in your detective's journal of everything you discover. It could be vital to your well-being, and helpful in solving the puzzles that await you.

Sincerest wishes,

Professor Hamatum-Sizzle

P.S. A taxi is waiting to take you to the airport.

1

THE SOBEK

'Welcome to the *Sobek*,' a young boy says, smiling as he beckons you up the gangplank of a gleaming white paddle steamer that's moored on the Nile.

Less than an hour ago, your plane touched down at Cairo airport. Even though you're still in the same time zone, Egypt feels like another world. At first your taxi raced along the dusty roads, past camels and palm trees. Then you came to a bustling market crammed with stalls, bazaars and emporiums, selling all kinds of spices, fruits and oils, and your driver began blaring the horn to clear a way through the carts and vendors selling cheap jewellery.

You slowed to a crawl. And just when you thought you were stuck, your driver took an abrupt turn and you came face to face with the pyramids. They're one of the world's greatest wonders. You never thought you'd see them first hand, and they're mesmerizing.

Then the taxi took another turn down a side street and they were gone.

As you pressed on, you opened the window to

cool down, but the arid air made it feel like you'd opened an oven. In the next breath you were reminded that Egypt is where the Nile famously bursts its banks, bringing life to the heart of the desert, creating the land of pharaohs and queens who built monumental temples and dynasties centuries before most countries had built villages.

It's a truly wondrous place. The desert dunes are an ocean of buried treasures and, as the Professor mentioned, mysteries and curses.

'I'm Abasi,' says the smiling boy as you reach the top of the gangplank. He's about your age. 'My father's the captain,' he continues, proudly patting the boat. 'The *Sobek* is named after the god of the Nile,' he explains. 'She's a hundred and fifty feet long, making her the longest boat on the river.' He leads you along the wooden walkway running round the boat. 'We call this the Boardwalk. The cabins are up front, away from the engines. We also have a Games Room, a Passenger Lounge and a private Dining Room. Up top is the Sundeck with a pool and loungers.'

'Where do you stay?' you ask, looking around.

'No one's asked me that before,' Abasi replies,

laughing, and covers his mouth with his hand. 'The crew sleep below deck. Between us, it's nice, but the real luxury is up here. The *Sobek* only sleeps eight people, so you can spread out.'

Your eyes open wide and you say, 'Only eight people on one ship?'

Abasi nods. 'They spared no expense – she's a thing of beauty.'

He's not wrong. Every brass rail running round the boat is gleaming in the late afternoon sunshine. You can't help marvelling at the polished decks as the stewards and chambermaids bustle about, preparing everything for the journey.

'I'll take your bag to your cabin,' Abasi says as you arrive at the Passenger Lounge, 'while you meet the other guests.'

'Thanks,' you say, handing over your suitcase. You hang on to your detective's satchel, just in case.

As you enter the Passenger Lounge, a loud voice says, 'Finally!'

You look round to see a skinny man standing at the bar. His nose and cheeks have the same purple tint as the wine he's drinking.

Standing beside him is a tall, elegant lady wearing

a headscarf covered in prints of exotic palm leaves and pineapples. 'Don't be rude, Gerald,' she says, and smiles at you.

'You tell him, Bridget,' remarks an older woman in a nearby armchair, who's fanning herself. Her evening dress is long and silky, like something a movie star would wear, and her necklace is home to the biggest diamond you've ever seen. Its sparkle is so bright, it must be real! The younger woman sitting beside her isn't half as glamorous. Her necklace looks like it came from one of the vendors in the market your taxi drove through. She's busy burying her head in a newspaper to ignore the conversation.

'All I meant, *Lady Hamilton*,' Gerald snaps back, 'was that now the last member of our party is here, we can *finally* get going.'

But the lady wearing the diamond necklace isn't interested.

Bridget turns to you and says, 'Please forgive my husband. We've been here a while.'

'We've been here all afternoon,' adds a lady playing backgammon.

'Lunch on the Boardwalk was lovely,' remarks her opponent, who has short dark hair and a pink neck scarf, and she rolls the dice.

'I'm sure it was, but we're not going anywhere until those damn stewards find my coat!' snorts an imposing man who's drinking whisky at another table.

'Oh for heaven's sake, Brigadier. The last thing you need here is a *coat*,' says the lady in the armchair as she continues to fan herself.

He turns on her with a scowl. 'It happens to be my *trench* coat.'

'Oh dear! I'm sure your military pension can afford to buy you another one,' the lady replies, rolling her eyes.

'Do I have to remind you of everything I sacrificed to get it, *Lady Hamilton*?' the man retorts.

'I'm no longer a *Lady*,' she replies with a sigh. 'And I've lost enough *things* through my divorce to know that things don't *really* matter.'

The woman sitting beside her tightens her grip, crumpling the newspaper. But her annoyance disappears as a stewardess arrives. For a moment the Brigadier's face fills with hope too, but it vanishes when he realizes the stewardess isn't carrying his trench coat.

The stewardess approaches the two ladies playing backgammon and holds out an envelope with a gold crest on the front. 'Miss Patti, there's a letter from your office in London,' she says.

The lady with the pink neck scarf takes it. 'Thank you. Does anyone have an opener?' she asks, glancing around the room.

No one replies so Lady Hamilton nudges her companion and says, 'Come along, Constance. Pay attention.'

Constance puts down her newspaper and starts rummaging through Lady Hamilton's handbag.

Lady Hamilton turns to Miss Patti. 'I get letters like that all time.'

Constance hands Miss Patti a silver letter opener. She thanks Constance, opens the letter and quickly scans it before slipping it into her jacket pocket. 'It's your move, Clara,' she says, and her opponent rolls the dice to resume their game.

As Clara moves her counters round the board, Miss Patti thoughtfully sips a glass of port. Then Constance spots you and gasps, 'Are you Arlo Banks?'

'Er, yes,' you reply.

Everyone in the lounge immediately stares at you, including the two women playing backgammon. Even Lady Hamilton stops fanning herself.

'The puzzle champion from the newspapers?' Gerald asks.

'I guess so,' you say, surprised that news of your travels has reached this corner of the world.

'A puzzle champion, you say?' the Brigadier enquires. 'Any chance you can figure out where my coat's disappeared to?'

'I'll try,' you reply.

'I'll drink to that,' Gerald says, and raises his wine as a toast to you.

'Good work on the Orient Express,' Miss Patti says. 'But do you think you could spot a cheat?'

Clara, her backgammon partner, scowls.

Most of the group quickly look away, repelled by Miss Patti's thinly veiled accusation, and Lady Hamilton eyes her from over her fan.

The awkwardness is interrupted by a blast from the boat's funnel. The Brigadier flinches like he's back in the trenches and spills his whisky down his shirt, and Lady Hamilton can't help laughing at his misfortune.

'Finally, we're off!' Gerald says, and downs his wine.

'We'd better unpack and freshen up for dinner,' Bridget says and leads Gerald out of the lounge.

'Good idea,' says the Brigadier, dabbing his shirt with a napkin and gets up.

'Come along, Constance, I feel like a swim before dinner,' Lady Hamilton announces, and her companion dutifully accompanies her out of the room.

'Oh, I'm ready for dinner,' Miss Patti says. 'Lunch was hours ago.'

As the rest of group depart, you consider your options . . .

If you decide to:

- **Visit the Games Room**, turn to **chapter 5**
- **Explore the ship**, turn to **chapter 2**

2

GAMES ON THE BOARDWALK

Palm trees and the deep azure sky reflect in the water as the brilliant white bow of the *Sobek* cuts through the Nile's sunlit ripples.

You wander along the Boardwalk, admiring the view, still struggling to believe that puzzle-solving has brought you to a paradise like this.

Abasi appears, carrying two shuffleboard paddles. 'Hello again,' he says. 'I was about to set these out. Would you like a game?'

'Sure,' you reply. 'But you'll have to teach me the rules.'

'It's easy,' Abasi replies and hands you a stack of black counters. He then places one of his yellow counters on the start line and shoves it down the play zone that's painted on the deck. In no time you're taking turns to shuffle counters and gather points.

'Having fun down there?' calls a voice from the Sundeck. You look up to see Lady Hamilton waving at you. As she cranes her neck to see your game, her diamond necklace catches the sunlight. 'Come on up. The water's very refreshing,' she says.

'We're good, thanks,' you reply, and continue the game.

You soon find out that you're surprisingly good at shuffleboard. But just as you start building a sizable lead, a gunshot rings out from the front of the boat.

To investigate, turn to **chapter 17**

3

THE GUN

'It must've been the gun – bullets kill every time,' you say, looking up at everyone.

'No they don't!' declares the Brigadier. 'And I should know; I fought in the Great War. If that's the sum total of your expertise, young man, I'm amazed you've made it this far!'

'Absolutely, there's a lot more to this than meets the eye,' Bridget says, nodding.

You turn and look again at Miss Patti's body – the pink scarf tightened round her neck and the foam on her lips. It must all mean something.

You open your detective's journal and write a list of clues. They seem quite cryptic, but they could reveal something you've missed.

Pure and simple.
Oddly effective.
It isn't for everyone.
Soon it might be, but it isn't.
Once is enough.
Never going back.

If you think she was killed by:

- **Poison**, turn to **chapter 8**
- **Her pink scarf**, turn to **chapter 10**

4

SHOCK ON THE SUNDECK

You run back along the Boardwalk and up the narrow stairs to the Sundeck. Lady Hamilton is standing in the centre of a huddled group, yelling.

'Here,' the Brigadier says, draping a towel over her shoulders.

'It's forty degrees!' Lady Hamilton snaps. 'I don't need a towel – I want my necklace.'

'It must be here somewhere,' Bridget tells her.

'It was, but it's not here now!' Lady Hamilton rages as she empties her handbag in search of her diamond necklace. Sunglasses, a powder compact, lipsticks, a purse and personal letters all get dumped on the deck. 'Those lawyers took everything,' she shouts. 'The house, my clothes, the paintings. Even my mother's jewellery. That necklace was all I had left. It was *my* inheritance!'

As Lady Hamilton continues her rant, Constance hurriedly gathers her things and stuffs them in a bag, but not before you notice a gold crest on one of her letters.

'Lady Hamilton, where did you last see your necklace?' you ask.

She turns on you like an angry cobra. 'You don't wear a diamond necklace like *that* in a swimming pool. I left it right here. Then all that horrid business happened in the cabin . . . I came back and it was gone!'

Cogs start turning in your head. 'OK. If the Scarab used the chaos caused by Miss Patti's murder as a distraction to steal the diamond necklace, they must've been ready for it. So the crimes must be connected.'

Everyone on the Sundeck stares at you.

'So now we have a murderer *and* a thief on board?' the Brigadier says.

'Two people, or one person – it could be either,' you reply. 'But first we need to establish their plan.'

You pull out your detective's journal and write a list of everything you know and piece together the Scarab's plan:

1. The Scarab knew that the poison would take time to work.
2. When Miss Patti was dead, they shot her to cover their tracks.
3. The shot brought everyone running to the cabin.
4. They used the shock and chaos to distract everyone.
5. And stole the necklace from the Sundeck.
6. They avoided being found at the cabin.
7. Stealing the necklace only took a minute.
8. They must've arrived with the rest of the group in Miss Patti's cabin after the shot was fired. So no one suspected them.

Now you have their plan, use your puzzling skills to work out how and where Miss Patti was poisoned so you can start searching for the murder weapon.

The foam on Miss Patti's lips and round her mouth told you she'd been poisoned, so you open your detective's journal and see if the poisons section can shed any light on which poison the killer used.

Helpful Facts About Poisons

Even though their outcomes are invariably the same, different poisons affect the human body in different ways.

Studying these effects, or symptoms as the medical profession refers to them, can help you determine which poison a victim has been exposed to, and even lead you to uncovering the method with which the poison was administered.

You scan the list of poisons and their effects and find three that could have caused Miss Patti to foam at the mouth.

Poisons

Sarin

Administered as a nerve gas. One breath and the victim will foam at the mouth, collapse into a coma and die.

Compound 1080

Developed as a farming drug. Odourless, tasteless, water-soluble and without antidote. Causes foaming at the mouth and a painful death in minutes.

Ricin

Found in castor beans, which can be innocently eaten. Respiratory failure and foaming at the mouth occur soon after consumption. Causes death hours later.

Clues

- Miss Patti's cabin is a confined space.
- She was drinking port as she played backgammon.
- Miss Patti and Clara ate lunch on the Boardwalk. That was hours ago so any evidence will have been cleared away by now, but a slow-acting poison could still work.
- Nothing was brought to her cabin, so if the poison was administered here it must've been in something she used, like soap or perfume.
- When you searched her cabin, nothing contained anything that smelt even slightly poisonous or showed signs of being tampered with.
- Miss Patti didn't seem ill in the Passenger Lounge and she was looking forward to dinner.
- If she was poisoned in the Passenger Lounge, it would implicate everyone who was in there.

Next you draw a grid in your detective's journal. Now go back through the poisons and your clues and use your powers of deduction to cross off the clues that contradict each other, tick the pieces of information that fit together, and use your conclusions to illuminate other details.

	EATING	DRINKING	USING	SARIN	COMPOUND 1080	RICIN
IN THE CABIN						
ON THE BOARDWALK						
IN THE PASSENGER LOUNGE						
SARIN						
COMPOUND 1080						
RICIN						

Now you can conclude that:

Miss Patti was poisoned by ____________________

something ____________________

spiked with ____________________

you can begin your search for the murder weapon.

If you think you should investigate:

- **The Passenger Lounge**, turn to **chapter 29**
- **Miss Patti's cabin**, turn to **chapter 6**
- **The Boardwalk**, turn to **chapter 27**

5

THE GAMES ROOM

As the ship prepares to set sail, you head along the Boardwalk to the Games Room. There's everything here: darts, billiards, another backgammon set, and a pale man in a white suit sitting at a chess table.

'Please,' he says, offering you the seat opposite.

'Thank you,' you reply.

'Many people think chess originated in India in the sixth century,' he replies, and slides a white pawn towards you to make the first move. 'But there are accounts – even tomb paintings – of chess being played in Egypt over five thousand years ago.'

'It's one big puzzle,' you say as the game gets underway.

'Indeed,' he replies. 'There's no element of chance in chess, so it's a battle of strategy and experience. But the secret is to always play your opponent, not their pieces. Look for their weaknesses and how you can use them to your advantage.'

You nod. 'And what's your weakness?'

He smiles at your directness. 'I don't like losing,' he replies.

With each move, the game progresses until you have a choice . . .

If you decide to:

- **Take his queen with your knight**, turn to **chapter 15**
- **Advance one of your pawns**, turn to **chapter 11**
- If you'd like to consider all your options, turn to the **next page** . . .

As you look at your pieces and their positions on the board, you realize you have a number of moves to choose from, and each one has a vastly different outcome.

Your bishop has a diagonal path that will put your opponent's king in check if they advance it or move it to the right. You could move it anywhere along that path, but since it can't take any of your opponent's pieces or change the game, it's best to stay put.

Your king is safe for now, flanked by your bishop and the adjacent rook. This rook also has a clear path to the opposite end of the board, but since it's currently preventing your opponent's king from moving left, you decide it's better off staying where it is until your opponent makes an aggressive move.

Your other rook is currently preventing your opponent's king from retreating, so it's serving a useful purpose and shouldn't move.

It all comes down to two moves: Your knight is in a prime position to take your opponent's queen, and when it does, nothing will be able to take it. This will put your opponent in checkmate and you will win the game.

It's a tantalizing move. But before you make it,

you look at your pawns. They're both on the right of the board. If you advance either one, your opponent's bishop will be able to take them, and you'll give your opponent's king a chance to avoid check.

It's your move.

If you need a little more help, you can always ask someone who plays chess!

If you decide to:

- **Take his queen with your knight**, turn to **chapter 15**
- **Move your pawn and sacrifice the game**, turn to **chapter 11**

6

MISS PATTI'S CABIN

You return to the cabin and start searching it – opening drawers, the wardrobe, the bedside cabinet. All you find are Miss Patti's belongings. Nothing contains anything that smells even slightly poisonous or shows any sign of being tampered with. She only brought a bar of soap in her wash bag and didn't use cosmetics or perfume.

As each lead proves to be a dead end, your confidence slips away.

The only thing that strikes you as odd are the scarab-carved beads from the broken bracelet lying across the floor. But they're hardly murder weapons so you knock them under the bed with a dismissive kick.

'It looks like you've drawn a blank,' the Brigadier says, reading your disappointment. 'Don't beat yourself up about it. Murder investigations require expertise and experience. No one was really expecting a youngster like you to come up trumps.'

He heads back to the Passenger Lounge, leaving you gazing at the passing dunes that were once ruled by great pharaohs and queens. You can't deny it, the Professor was right: *Egypt is a country full of ancient mysteries that have been lost in the sands of the desert and time . . .*

As much as it pains you to admit it, the Brigadier was right too. And Miss Patti's murder and the theft of Lady Hamilton's diamond necklace are two more mysteries that will never be solved. As a sad smile finds its way on to your face, you know it's time to hang up your detective's kit and head for home.

THE END

7

THE DEATH OF CLARA

The huge rock smacks into the ground, cracking the stone floor with a deadening thud. The impact throws up a dust cloud that engulfs the whole group.

You crouch down, instinctively clutching your head, and a stunned silence fills the temple.

Something scuttles over your foot. A flap of fabric slaps your back and disappears into the dust cloud. You get up and stumble around, looking for the others. But all you find is more dust.

Seconds or minutes pass, you can't tell which. The swirling, gritty air catches in your throat, making you cough and splutter. Running feet pound the ground around you, desperate to escape.

Then a woman screams in horror.

As the dust begins to settle, you discover the situation is far worse than you feared.

Clara's body is lying at the foot of a towering stone pillar. She's been stabbed. The wound is short and thin, but there's blood everywhere so it must've gone deep enough to kill her.

As more of the dust clouds clear, something else is revealed.

Clara didn't die immediately, so she had time to leave a clue, written in blood on one column carved with hieroglyphics.

You remember the tour guide explaining that hieroglyphics are circled to signify someone's name. You take out your detective's journal and open the section on translations.

Use the guide below to decode the hieroglyphics Clara circled and see if you can find the name of whoever Clara believed attacked her. But be warned: Clara was desperate and dying in a dust cloud, so the clues might need some interpretation.

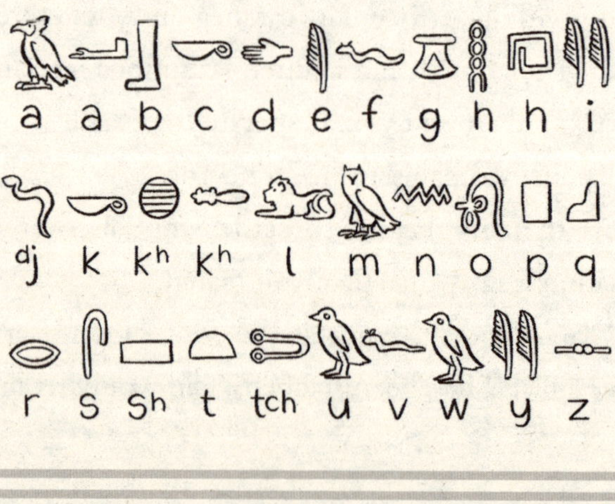

If you think you've found the name:

- **Bridget**, turn to **chapter 32**
- **Brigadier**, turn to **chapter 33**

8

THE POISON

'She was poisoned,' you tell everyone, pointing to the foam round her mouth. 'Bullets and scarves work fast. If Miss Patti had been shot or strangled *before* the poison could work, the foam wouldn't be here. And her body would still be warm.'

'So we have a poisoner on board,' says the Brigadier.

Everyone in the cabin starts eyeing each other with suspicion, but your eye is drawn to one of the beads you found rolling around on the floor and you focus on its engraving of a scarab. You pick it up with a match and slip it in an evidence bag.

'Does this mean anything to any of you?' you ask, holding up the bead.

'Who cares about those ghastly things? They're always scuttling about the place, spreading germs and filthy diseases,' Lady Hamilton says with a shiver, and Constance shakes her head.

'They're everywhere in Egypt,' Bridget says. 'They're carved in temples and even hide in the sand. It's quite a fascination.'

'My book says scarabs were part of ancient Egyptian burial rituals,' Clara explains.

'An association with death,' the Brigadier muses, thinking out loud.

You nod as your thoughts take shape: *Ghastly things associated with death, scuttling about the place, spreading germs and filthy diseases . . . The poisoner on board has quite a lot in common with scarabs.*

Your Scarab, however, might think they can hide in the shadows and scuttle around poisoning people, but you'll see about that!

You slip the evidence bag containing the carved bead into your satchel for safekeeping and focus your thoughts on how you're going to catch *the Scarab*.

'Poor Patti,' Clara says, sniffing back tears. 'She never hurt anyone.'

'Didn't she accuse you of cheating?' Gerald asks.

Clara glares at him. 'Never!'

'Yes she did!' Bridget adds. 'Don't you remember – she asked Arlo if he could spot a cheater.'

'She wasn't talking about *me*!' Clara declares. 'That was just a bit of . . . professional needling.'

'*Professional needling?*' you say, frowning with intrigue.

'Yes. We're insurance lawyers. It's our job to track down cheats and fraudsters,' Clara explains.

'Well, she isn't a lawyer any more,' Lady Hamilton remarks, but only she finds that funny. Constance silences her with a gentle nudge.

As you look around for more clues, the Captain arrives and the Brigadier fills him in on everything you've established.

'My goodness,' the Captain says with a shudder. 'Who could've done such a thing?'

'That's what I plan to find out,' you reply.

'Please do!' he says, nodding as he shakes your hand. 'If there's anything my crew can do to help, just ask.'

'Thank you,' you reply. That reminds you of the letter Miss Patti received in the Passenger Lounge. It's still in her jacket pocket, so you carefully remove it.

'Well, whoever this *poisoner* is, they must be somewhere on board,' says the Brigadier. 'I suggest we all return to our cabins and keep safe for the time being.'

As soon as you're safely inside your cabin, you sit down at the writing desk, open your detective's journal and write up your notes from the scene of

Miss Patti's murder. Then you open Miss Patti's letter. Printed at the top is the same gold crest that was on the envelope.

From the offices of Mortan & Flinn

Dear Miss Patti,

I hope everything is going swimmingly in Egypt.

Here's a quick update on the latest developments here in England. The fate of the family's country estate has now been finalized and the sale will proceed in due course. This should not affect the situation over there, or your special mission, but we thought you ought to be aware, since all information can prove to be useful.

Please inform Clara. And for heaven's sake, keep your eyes peeled. Anything could happen out there.

Yours,

Reginald Flinn,
Senior Partner

You sit there for a minute, wondering what it could all mean.

What was the 'special mission' Miss Patti's bosses sent her on?

And what situation here could be affected by the sale of a family's country estate back in England?

Whatever was behind the letter's cryptic message, Miss Patti didn't seem bothered when she read it in the Passenger Lounge. All the same, there's every chance it has something to do with her murder.

As you try to work out what might be going on, a horrified scream comes from the Sundeck.

Turn to **chapter 4**

9

FOLLOWING CONSTANCE

The sun rises over the southern city of Luxor. The *Sobek* is moored at a jetty a short walk from one of the grandest temples in Egypt – the Temple of Ammon.

Breakfast is served in your cabin, and after making your plan for the day, you join the others on the Boardwalk for the excursion. Lady Hamilton keeps everyone waiting. She arrives without an apology. Constance is lagging behind her, sweating under the weight of a large handbag.

'Oh, Constance, dear. You don't look at all well,' Lady Hamilton remarks. 'Why don't you stay behind?'

'Thank you, Your Ladyship. If you don't mind carrying your bag?' she replies.

'I don't carry the bags!' Lady Hamilton snaps, shooing Constance away with a wave of her fan.

'Here, let me help,' you say.

To your surprise, Constance pulls the bag away from you. 'Do you mind? These are Lady Hamilton's personal belongings!' she says.

'Quite right, Constance,' Lady Hamilton snaps. 'We can't have just anyone handling them. It's that kind of lax attitude that led to my necklace being stolen. You're not the thief, are you?'

'No!' you reply, thinking fast before you reveal your suspicions. 'I was only offering to help.'

'A likely story!' Lady Hamilton huffs, casting a suspicious eye over you.

'It's all right, I can manage, thank you,' Constance says, and skulks back to her cabin.

'Well that's settled then. Come along, everyone,' Lady Hamilton says, and leads the group off the boat. As much as you want to stay and keep an eye on Constance, the Brigadier beckons you to join the others.

Turn to **chapter 25**

10

THE PINK NECKSCARF

'She was strangled,' you say, looking up at everyone.

'What nonsense,' barks the Brigadier. 'Look at her neck! Strangling leaves marks. Where are the bruises?' He shakes his head.

You reach down and pull back the neck scarf. There are no marks on Patti's neck so you turn her body over and check the underneath. She's heavier than you expect, and turning her takes all your strength. And in turning her over, you smudge the foam on her lips, get her blood on your clothes and disturb how and where she fell.

To cap it all, as you take off her scarf you realize the Brigadier was right all along. There are no marks of any kind on Miss Patti's neck.

You immediately feel very silly.

'It's such a mess. Why would anyone do this?' Clara asks, crying into her hands. 'I mean, poison *and* shoot her?'

'It's all right. Solving murders is a job for the

police,' says the Brigadier, and he tries to console Clara while your face burns with embarrassment. 'And now Arlo has contaminated the crime scene, they'll have their work cut out!'

A sense of shame hits you like a lightning bolt. By wrecking the crime scene, you've ruined every trace left by the killer.

You place Miss Patti's body back where you found it, but it's too late. Your fingerprints are all over her scarf and the scarab beads you picked up. You've even managed to get her blood on your hands and everything you've touched!

Before long, the police arrive and sure enough, they find your fingerprints all over the scene. You protest your innocence, but even though Abasi was with you when the gun went off, they refuse to listen. You're led away in handcuffs, leaving everyone else to enjoy the rest of their holiday with a stone-cold murderer on board.

THE END

11

A CURIOUS ENCOUNTER

'That's very courteous of you,' the man says as you advance your pawn. He could take it with his bishop, but instead he takes your knight with his rook and puts you in checkmate.

You smile and shake his outstretched hand. 'Thank you, Arlo,' he says. 'That was a game very well played. And I know you could've won.'

You don't remember telling him your name, but now it seems impolite to ask his.

'I should unpack and prepare for dinner,' you say, making an excuse and getting up.

'Of course,' the man replies, checking his watch. 'I also have a plane to catch.'

'Aren't you on the tour?' you enquire.

The man shakes his head. 'No. But I have a feeling our paths will cross again before too long.'

You head to your cabin with the intention of unpacking, but the sight of the luxurious bed, with its soft cotton sheets and feather pillows, makes you feel an overwhelming wave of tiredness and you can't resist lying down.

In less than a minute, you're fast asleep, dreaming about a maze filled with puzzles.

You're awoken by a gunshot.

You sit bolt upright, instantly awake and alert.

Was it part of your dream? you wonder.

The running feet thundering along the Boardwalk tell a different story – one that's terrifyingly real – so you rush to investigate . . .

Turn to **chapter 17**

12

COBRA B

You grab the towel and shake out the folded cobra. There's nothing inside it, nor anything that seems odd. So you breathe a sigh of relief and tell yourself it's only natural to be suspicious when you're on a boat with a murderer.

You take the towel into the bathroom. As you turn on the faucet, a shadowy figure steps out from behind the door and grabs you. The running water hides the sound of your struggles . . . the smashing mirror . . . the breaking cabinet . . .

A few days later your body washes up downstream. It's assumed that you drowned while taking a pre-dinner swim in the Nile, but the truth of your demise will never be known.

THE END

13

THE EMPTY COURTYARD

You follow the twisting, narrow passageways through the temple. The suspect gradually gets away from you, and you know you've truly lost them when you find the trench coat lying abandoned on the floor. The woollen material is a heavy khaki-green, and the gold that glinted in the sunlight indicates it was worn by a high-ranking soldier.

This must be the Brigadier's missing trench coat!

You pick it up and a small bead engraved with a scarab falls out of the pocket. You instantly recognize it. And more importantly, it's proof that connects the coat with Miss Patti's murder.

So that leaves the question: *Who was wearing it?*

And you think you know . . .

A wave of urgency rises inside you. You grab the bead and the coat and make your way out of the temple.

By the time you emerge, the sun has moved to

the far side of the courtyard. The local police have arrived and are busy checking the fallen block and recording the crime scene round Clara's body.

It will take them weeks to find all the clues you have in your detective's journal, and by then whoever is responsible for the murders and stole Lady Hamilton's diamond necklace will be long gone.

Instead of spending the rest of the day helping the police with their enquiries, you hurry back to the *Sobek*.

Abasi is waiting for you. 'Oh, thank God. My dad was about to send out a search party for you.'

'Sorry,' you say. 'Where is everyone?'

'They're in the Passenger Lounge. Why?'

'I have everything I need to explain who took Lady Hamilton's diamond necklace and killed Miss Patti, Clara and Gerald,' you say, sounding confident.

'You'd better go straight there,' Abasi says.

Turn to **chapter 40**

ANOTHER BLOCK

Your fingers grip the edges of the large square block and pull it back. The rocks above instantly fall down, filling the gap you were hoping to crawl through.

But the situation is no longer as dark as it seemed.

The rest of the rockfall stays in place, giving you one more chance at removing a block to escape, but you can sense it's teetering on total collapse. Look again at the other two blocks and the rubble above them and see if removing them will give you an opening to escape through.

Make sure you choose wisely!

If you remove:

- **Block A**, turn to **chapter 34**
- **Block B**, turn to **chapter 22**

15

PLAYING TO THE END

'Well played,' the man says as you swap your knight for his queen and put him in checkmate. 'But you failed to spot one thing.'

You frown at him, confused, certain that all your pieces are in the right places.

'You played the game all right,' he says. 'But you didn't play me.' His eyes stare into yours. 'I told you I didn't like losing.'

You open your mouth to defend yourself. But before you can get the words out, he shoots you with a poison dart he's been hiding under the table.

An icy numbness sweeps through your body and you slump down on the floor.

The man gets up and calmly slips the dart-gun inside his jacket. A cruel look twists his face. 'I'm glad we met, Arlo. Some people know me as the White King,' he says. 'You can take my queen and all my other pieces, but you'll never take me.'

As he strides away, you slip into a state of unconsciousness and never wake up.

THE END

FOLLOWING LADY HAMILTON

The sun rises over the southern city of Luxor. The *Sobek* is moored at a jetty a short walk from one of the grandest temples in Egypt – the Temple of Ammon.

Breakfast is served in your cabin, and after making your plan for the day, you join the others on the Boardwalk for the excursion. Lady Hamilton keeps everyone waiting. She arrives without an apology. Constance is lagging behind her, sweating under the weight of a large handbag.

'Oh, Constance, dear. You don't look at all well,' Lady Hamilton remarks. 'Why don't you stay behind?'

'Thank you, Your Ladyship. If you don't mind carrying your bag?' she replies.

'I don't carry the bags!' Lady Hamilton snaps, shooing Constance away with a wave of her fan.

'Here, let me help,' you say.

To your surprise, Constance pulls the bag away

from you. 'Do you mind? These are Lady Hamilton's personal belongings!'

'Quite right, Constance,' Lady Hamilton snaps. 'We can't have just anyone handling them. It's that kind of lax attitude that led to my necklace being stolen. You're not the thief, are you?'

'No!' you reply.

'It's all right, Lady Hamilton. I don't think Arlo meant to ruffle any feathers,' the Brigadier says.

'Well, come along, everyone. We haven't got all day,' Lady Hamilton says with a swipe of her fan and leads the group off the boat, leaving Constance to skulk back to her cabin.

Turn to **chapter 25**

17

THE KILLING IN THE CABIN

The gunshot shattered the peaceful calm of the river and people are running from all across the boat to find out what's going on.

You join them and race to the front of the boat and arrive to find a cabin door hanging open. You peer inside and discover that something awful has happened to Miss Patti. She's lying on the floor of her cabin, her legs and arms at awkward angles where she collapsed. A bracelet of beads that must've come from a street vendor is lying broken beside her. The beads are carved with a scarab design you find on temples and statues.

But why is this here? you wonder.

As you check for Miss Patti's pulse and realize her body is cold, Abasi asks, 'Is she dead?'

You nod slowly and the sadness of finding another body rolls in like the tide.

As you take out your detective's journal and start

making careful notes of the scarab beads and other details of the scene, a crowd gathers at the door. Gerald is first to appear, closely followed by Bridget, the Brigadier and Constance. Lady Hamilton arrives in a robe, dripping pool water on the deck boards.

Clara, Miss Patti's backgammon partner, bursts in and screams in shock. She rushes to help her friend but the Brigadier holds her back. 'There's nothing you can do,' he tells her.

'I only left her a few minutes ago. She wanted to have a lie-down before dinner while I read my Egypt book,' Clara says with a sob.

'She's been shot,' you say, pointing to the wound in Miss Patti's chest. 'But that's not her only injury. Her scarf is wound so tightly round her neck she could've been strangled. There's also foam on her lips.'

'Yes. That looks like she was poisoned,' comments the Brigadier.

'Maybe,' you say, nodding. Either way, whoever did this wanted her dead, so the question is: Which method killed her?

You focus on Clara. 'I know this is hard for you, but anything you can tell me about the last few hours might be helpful.'

Clara nods and dries her eyes. 'We got here around midday and ate lunch on the Boardwalk. We had the whole boat to ourselves. It was lovely,' she says. 'Eventually it became too hot out there, so we moved to the Passenger Lounge and spent the afternoon playing backgammon, waiting for everyone else to arrive. It was her favourite game.'

'Thank you,' you say and turn to a blank page in your detective's journal. You begin by listing the potential ways Miss Patti could've been killed and a few notes about them.

The Murder Methods That Killed Miss Patti

- Shot with a gun – bullets kill in an instant.
- Poisoned – even the fastest poison takes more than a few minutes to take effect.
- Strangled with her pink neck scarf – it would take just a few seconds.

Then you draw a timeline that runs from when Miss Patti arrived on board all the way to when she was shot just a minute ago.

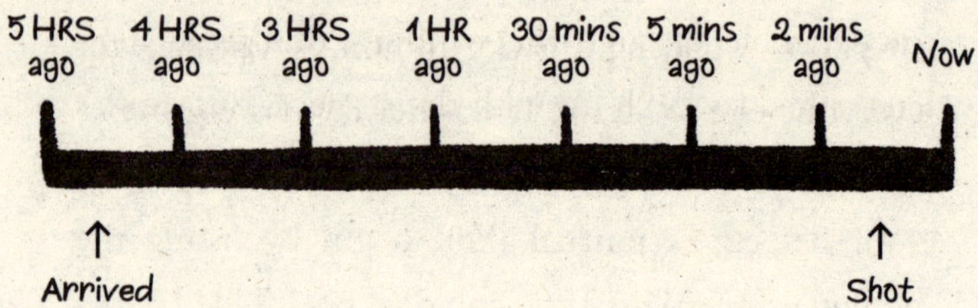

Using the timeline and your notes, mark your estimations of how long it would've taken the poison and the pink neck scarf to kill Miss Patti. Then see if you can deduce which is the most likely murder weapon.

If you think it was:

- **The gun**, turn to **chapter 3**
- **The poison**, turn to **chapter 8**
- **The pink neck scarf,** turn to **chapter 10**

18

THE TOP OF THE TEMPLE

You scramble through the winding, dusty tunnels, determined to catch up with the suspect. But every time you think you're getting close, the tunnel takes a twist or a block in the uneven floor trips you up, and they get away.

You keep after them, running at every chance and not even stopping to rub your bruises. Eventually the dry desert heat and the scent of the Nile mix with the musty air that's been trapped in here for centuries, and you emerge at the top of the temple.

The glaring sun hits you. As your eyes try to adjust, you squint through your hands and see a figure at the far end, standing with their back to the dazzling sun.

It could be the Brigadier. But then again, it could not. You can't tell.

'It's all right,' you call out.

As you approach the figure, you realize that all the tourists who fled the temple are now crowded in the courtyard below. The sound of your voice makes them look up.

The figure responds with a solemn shake of their head.

There's a chance you can grab their hand and pull them back from the edge. You just need to take one more step towards them . . .

You go for it, but they instantly recoil.

Then they slip.

Horror fills your body as they fall with a flutter of the trench coat.

You can't bear to watch.

The next few seconds become a memory that haunts you for the rest of your life.

After so many onlookers testify that you pushed the mysterious figure off the top of the temple, it takes the courts less than an hour to find you guilty of murder. The Egyptian police have no trouble pinning the other murders on you too, so you spend the rest of your life in an Egyptian prison wondering what happened to Lady Hamilton's diamond necklace . . .

THE END

19

FOLLOWING CLARA

The sun rises over the southern city of Luxor. The *Sobek* is moored at a jetty a short walk from one of the grandest temples in Egypt – the Temple of Ammon.

Breakfast is served in your cabin, and after making your plan for the day, you join the others on the Boardwalk for the excursion. Clara seems well rested, as though her glass of port helped her sleep. Lady Hamilton keeps everyone waiting. She arrives without an apology. Constance is lagging behind her, sweating under the weight of a large handbag.

'Oh, Constance, dear. You don't look at all well,' Lady Hamilton remarks. 'Why don't you stay behind?'

'Thank you, Your Ladyship. If you don't mind carrying your bag?' she replies.

'I don't carry the bags!' Lady Hamilton snaps, shooing Constance away with a wave of her fan.

'Come along, everyone,' she says, and leads the group off the boat, leaving Constance to skulk back to her cabin.

The Great Temple of Ammon is a huge, sprawling ruin of sandstone blocks and carved sphinxes, statues and hieroglyphics. The tour guide leads the group through the temple and stops beside a statue of Amun-Ra, the one-time chief god of Egypt. You muscle yourself into a position between Clara and Bridget at the foot of a towering column and pretend to listen intently as Clara asks the kind of questions that someone with a keen interest in Egypt would want to know.

You don't hear the scraping of a block being pushed towards the edge of a column high above you. The scrape as it teeters on the brink is lost in the gentle breeze, and the gritty sand particles that break away fall soundlessly into the air. The block drops, plummeting in silence, building in speed, as the tour guide tells you how the temple has stood here for over three thousand years . . .

The first thing you're aware of is a looming shadow and rushing air. The sensation lasts barely a fleeting moment before the block lands on you. The force of the impact even cracks the stone ground beneath your feet.

After a short investigation the police conclude that your death was an unfortunate accident. And on this trip, it won't be the last.

THE END

TYRE TRACK OPTION B

As soon as you start following the tyre tracks, you realize you've chosen the right set. They lead you straight out of the car park and back to the main road.

In no time they've merged with the tracks left by cars, motorbikes and the camels that trek through here. But it doesn't matter. You know you're heading in the right direction, and before long, you start seeing signposts that lead you back to Luxor.

You reach the Temple of Ammon, exhausted from the long walk. Luckily there are stalls selling water, so you stop off to refresh yourself, and your thoughts return to your search for the Scarab.

As you approach the *Sobek*, you find Abasi sitting on the jetty looking sad. 'There you are,' he says, without his usual friendly warmth.

'What's going on?' you ask, concerned.

He leans in close and says in a hushed voice, 'When everyone returned without you, my dad asked the group to wait in the Passenger Lounge and sent a couple of stewards to search the Valley of the Kings. When they couldn't find you, we called the police. But by then everyone else was dead – they were poisoned in the Passenger Lounge. Constance survived, but she's very sick. Since you weren't there, the police want to talk to you.'

Shock fills your face. 'How did that happen?' you ask.

'The police think you know,' Abasi replies with a grave expression. 'You'd better come with me.'

THE END

21

THE SCORPION

With each twist and turn of the tunnel you lose your sense of direction. You're so determined to catch up with the suspect, you don't realize you've taken a wrong turn until it gets so dark you run into a solid stone wall. You turn round, feeling your way with your fingertips. But all you find is one block of stone after another.

Frustration sets in and you start slapping your hands against the stone walls. Instead of finding a gap in the stone, you feel a sharp burning sensation. You think it's an old nail, but the pain enters your bloodstream and races up your arm like a bolt of lightning.

Years later your body is found. You've been slowly mummified by the desert heat, so it's easy for the archaeologists to conclude that you were stung by a deadly scorpion.

By then, Lady Hamilton, her missing necklace and even the three unsolved murders that took place on your trip have all passed out of living memory – along with your disappearance.

THE END

22

WAITING FOR A RESCUE

Removing the block is simple enough, but as soon as it comes out, you cause another rockfall. Dozens of stone blocks tumble down, sealing the hole you were expecting to crawl through and robbing you of any chance of getting out.

You sit there in the tunnel, feeling stunned. When the last of your matches burns out, you resign yourself to waiting, in the hope of being rescued.

Time passes and the sweltering heat begins to feel like you're trapped in an oven. You sweat until your head pounds. You've never felt so thirsty. Bright lights start to flash in the darkness, like chinks of sunlight shining between the rocks. But each time you reach out for them, your fingers find the solid pile of fallen stones. You soon realize you're hallucinating, and eventually you pass out.

Weeks later, when the rescue team reopen the tomb, they're shocked to find your bone-dry body lying in the tunnel. Your fingers are worn to the bone from your desperate attempts to dig your way out through the solid rock.

The authorities conclude that the rockfall was unfortunate. But out there somewhere is a person who knows different. They wanted you dead, as much as they wanted Lady Hamilton's diamond necklace. It's just a shame that their identity, along with the truth, will never be known.

THE END

RETURN TO THE SOBEK

Your trip across the desert has left you dehydrated and dizzy. It's a huge relief to be back at the *Sobek*. Waiting on a coffee table at the top of the gang-ramp is a jug of water and some glasses. A few have been drunk from, so you help yourself to a clean one and pour out a cool glass of water.

You've never missed water so much. You immediately pour yourself another glass and down it. As the cooling sensation trickles through your chest, you look around, wondering where everyone is.

Are they in the Passenger Lounge, or relaxing on the Sundeck?

You set off to look for them, but you don't get very far.

Agony tears out from your stomach into your internal organs. You collapse on the Boardwalk and realize you're foaming at the mouth.

You call out and footsteps come running.

Someone emerges from the Passenger Lounge. They're shocked and surprised to see you lying there. But your vision is blurring and even though the sun is still beating down, you feel cold and everything is turning dark.

Your body is never found and neither is your killer. Curiously, Lady Hamilton's diamond necklace is found some years later. But the finder has no idea how it arrived in London, the history behind it or how it came into the possession of the seller. All they know is: don't ask questions when their answers could get you killed.

THE END

24

FOLLOWING THE BRIGADIER

You don't sleep much that night. Instead, you gaze out of your cabin window at the moonlight dancing on the Nile while your thoughts refuse to rest.

The sun rises over the southern city of Luxor. The *Sobek* is moored at a jetty a short walk from one of the grandest temples in Egypt – the Temple of Ammon.

Breakfast is served in your cabin, and after making your plan for the day, you join the others on the Boardwalk for the excursion. The Brigadier is unusually quiet. The look in his eye reminds you of the thousand-yard stare soldiers get when they've been fighting for too long.

Lady Hamilton keeps everyone waiting. She arrives without an apology. Constance is lagging behind her, sweating under the weight of a large handbag.

'Oh, Constance, dear. You don't look at all well,' Lady Hamilton remarks. 'Why don't you stay behind?'

'Thank you, Your Ladyship. If you don't mind carrying your bag?' she replies.

'I don't carry the bags!' Lady Hamilton snaps, shooing Constance away with a wave of her fan. 'Come along, everyone,' she says, and leads the group off the boat, leaving Constance to skulk back to her cabin.

Turn to **chapter 25**

25

THE GREAT TEMPLE

The Great Temple of Ammon is a huge, sprawling ruin of sandstone blocks and carved sphinxes and statues. Your tour guide relays its history as they lead the group through the temple to the central nave. It's a forest of towering stone columns, each one carved with intricate hieroglyphics that loom larger than the tallest trees on Earth. Even by today's standards, the engineering and artistry are mind-blowing. But you're not here to marvel at the craftsmanship.

Your tour guide stops beside a statue of Amun-Ra, the one-time chief god of Egypt. The Brigadier listens intently while Clara asks the kind of questions that someone with a keen interest in Egypt would want to know. Lady Hamilton looks around, fanning herself with an air of interest. Bridget is going along with this, but her thoughts are clearly elsewhere.

You don't hear the scraping of a block being pushed towards the edge of a column high above you.

The scrape as it teeters on the brink is lost in the gentle breeze, and the gritty sand particles that break away fall soundlessly into the air. The block drops, plummeting in silence, building in speed, as the tour guide tells you how the temple stood here for over three thousand years . . .

Turn to **chapter 7**

THE TOWELS IN THE CABIN

No matter how many times you look at the pieces of broken glass, you can't see any way for them to fit together. Eventually you give up and return to your cabin.

You open the door to find that your luggage has been unpacked. Your pyjamas have been laid out on your pillow and an outfit for tonight's dinner is hanging on the wardrobe door. As strange as it seems to have dinner while there's a murderer on board, this might give you a chance to catch them. So you decide to have a shower to wake yourself up and sharpen your senses before you sit down with everyone.

The stewards have folded your towels into the shapes of two king cobras facing each other on your bed. They do this for all the guests, but you can still sense there's something oddly different about them.

Can you spot what it is?

A

B

If you think there's something oddly different about:

- **Cobra A**, turn to **chapter 39**
- **Cobra B**, turn to **chapter 12**

27

THE BOARDWALK

As soon as you set foot on the Boardwalk, you almost slip on the pool water that dripped off Lady Hamilton. You crouch down low and study the polished wooden boards, using the sunlight to highlight any marks that could be a clue. Besides the drips left by Lady Hamilton and a few scuffs from the crew, there's nothing.

'So Miss Patti walked along here and went straight to her cabin?' you ask.

'Yes,' Clara replies, sniffing back her tears.

'And no insects bit her? No blow darts were fired at her? She didn't react to anything?' you ask.

'No!' Clara says. 'There was nothing.'

'Arlo, I believe you're clutching at straws,' the Brigadier says.

'Maybe. But Miss Patti must've been poisoned somewhere on board this boat,' you say.

Adamant that you can still solve this and catch the Scarab, you open your detective's journal . . .

Look back over the clues that have led you here and see if you can work out where Miss Patti was poisoned.

If you think she was poisoned:

- **In the Passenger Lounge**, turn to **chapter 29**
- **Her cabin**, turn to **chapter 6**

28

FOLLOWING BRIDGET

The sun rises over the southern city of Luxor. The *Sobek* is moored at a jetty a short walk from one of the grandest temples in Egypt – the Temple of Ammon.

Breakfast is served in your cabin, and after making your plan for the day, you join the others on the Boardwalk for the excursion. Bridget arrives, looking like she hasn't slept. You say good morning and smile so it doesn't seem strange that you'll be staying close to her on the excursion.

Lady Hamilton keeps everyone waiting. She arrives without an apology. Constance is lagging behind her, sweating under the weight of a large handbag.

'Oh, Constance, dear. You don't look at all well,' Lady Hamilton remarks. 'Why don't you stay behind?'

'Thank you, Your Ladyship. If you don't mind

carrying your bag?' she replies.

'I don't carry the bags!' Lady Hamilton snaps, shooing Constance away with a wave of her fan. 'Come along everyone,' she says, and leads the group off the boat, leaving Constance to skulk back to her cabin.

Turn to **chapter 25**

29

THE PASSENGER LOUNGE

You head to the Passenger Lounge to begin your search for whatever poisoned Miss Patti. Your thoughts churn as you hurry along the Boardwalk. *If she was poisoned on the ship, then the murderer must also be on board. So there isn't a moment to lose.*

You arrive to find the tables and chairs have been neatly arranged round the tables by the stewardess who manages the bar.

You stop just inside the entrance and let the doors close behind you, re-creating your first arrival. Casting your mind back, you recall where everyone else was sitting, and in the cases of Gerald and Bridget, standing at the bar. Lady Hamilton and Constance were sitting at a table near the Brigadier as he sulked about his missing coat, while Clara and Miss Patti played backgammon. The board is now closed and the dice and counters have been put away.

As you run through the conversation, you recall

the stewardess arriving with the letter for Miss Patti and that Miss Patti was drinking . . .

A glass of port.

You go behind the bar. Usually, a young boy wouldn't be allowed anywhere near these bottles, but this is an exception.

One by one you check the bottles lined up on a shelf.

The only bottle of port here is full – sealed and brand new.

As you look around to see if it's been put somewhere else, the stewardess arrives. 'Can I help you?' she asks.

'Maybe,' you reply. 'Can you tell me where the bottle of port has gone?'

The stewardess scans the shelf of bottles. 'If it's not here, someone must've drunk it.'

Someone did – *it was Miss Patti and she paid for it with her life!*

'The empty bottles are in the bin down there,' the stewardess says, pointing under the bar.

You look down and sure enough there's a bin full of empty bottles, but they're broken.

'Hey, you can't do that,' the stewardess says as you

start dragging the bin out from behind the bar. But before she can stop you, you empty the whole broken lot on the floor.

'Do I have to call the Captain?' she exclaims.

'If you want,' you reply, opening your satchel. 'But this could be vital to a murder investigation.' You take out your detective's journal as well as a pouch containing a small set of litmus papers and a bottle of liquid with a dropper fitted in the cap.

The stewardess frowns at you. 'I hope you know what you're doing!'

'I have good reason to believe that one of these bottles contains the poison that killed Miss Patti. And if I can find the port bottle, this clever little test kit could prove it,' you explain.

The stewardess looks bewildered, but she doesn't stop you as you crouch down and start examining the pieces of broken glass, taking care not to step on any of them.

If you can put the pieces from all the broken bottles back together, there's a chance you'll find the port bottle and you might find the murder weapon.

If you:

- **Can't put the bottles back together**, turn to **chapter 26**
- **Decide to test all of the pieces of glass with your poison-detecting kit**, turn to **chapter 30**
- **Can't find the port bottle**, turn to **chapter 36**

THE CLEVER LITTLE SPOT TEST

Rather than take the time to piece the bottles back together, you decide to try something else. You open your detective's journal and find the instructions for the spot test.

How To Detect A Poison

Many substances can be poisonous if they are given in a large enough quantity. But the more harmful poisons, preferred by assassins and killers around the world, are fiercely toxic.

This simple test will determine whether a given substance is in fact a poison:

1. If the given substance is a powder, dissolve it in water. If the substance is a liquid, skip this step.

2. Add two drops of liquid from the bottle provided in the test kit to the substance.

3. Shake the mixture and wait one minute.

4. If the mixture turns blue, you've found a lethal poison.

You spend the next ten minutes dripping the solution from the bottle in your test kit on to the pieces of broken glass. But none of them turn blue. The only interesting thing to happen is the solution turns the red wine left on one of the bottles clear.

But besides that, the tests don't find any traces of poison.

You let out a defeated sigh and the stewardess asks, 'Are you sure the bottle you're after is even there?'

You look back at the broken pieces and realize the stewardess might be right. So you start piecing the bottles back together . . .

If you:

- **Can't put the bottles back together**, turn to **chapter 26**
- **Can't find the port bottle**, turn to **chapter 36**

31

TYRE TRACK OPTION A

You refuse to discount this set of tyre tracks, but try as you might, you can't find where they lead to. Round and round the car park you go, following the tyre tracks, until a voice calls out, 'Hey my friend. Are you OK?'

You look up to see a smiling Egyptian man with a white head scarf and a long cream robe. It's the perfect outfit for the intense desert heat.

'Hi,' you say, and wave back with a smile.

He hurries over and hands you a bottle of water. 'Here, my friend,' he says, as you open the bottle and start guzzling. 'It's not good to be out in this heat. Come with me. I have a little shop over here. I'll give you more water and somewhere to cool off.'

'Thank you,' you say, and he leads you to a little stone building by the roadside, a short walk from the car park.

Inside, the walls are covered with shelves crammed full of things to buy. Even the ceiling has hooks and racks, all dripping with souvenirs and trinkets.

'Please, you want to buy something?' he asks as your eyes try to take it all in.

If you:

- **Would like to buy something**, turn to **chapter 37**
- **Don't want to buy anything**, turn to **chapter 38**

32

THE VALLEY OF THE KINGS

As the dust clouds settle, you decode the last of the hieroglyphics. From what you can gather, the letters Clara circled spell the name 'Bridget'.

This won't be enough to persuade the local police to arrest her. You decide to keep this to yourself for the time being, so you shut your detective's journal, and make your way out of the temple.

In the courtyard you find the Brigadier, Bridget and Lady Hamilton gathered with the tour guide near a statue of a sphinx. They all look shocked by Clara's death – apart from Lady Hamilton. 'I vote we continue the tour to the Valley of the Kings,' she says.

'Really?' you ask, struggling to believe that anyone would want to visit tombs straight after someone has died.

'Well, you only come to a place like this once in a lifetime. I'm not wasting the opportunity to see everything,' Lady Hamilton replies, waving her fan.

The Brigadier opens his mouth to say something, but Bridget stops him. 'Come on,' she says. 'This business is so awful, I could do with a distraction.'

The Brigadier relents and the tour guide leads you all to a bus.

The bus takes you along a dusty road out of the city to the Valley of the Kings. You keep a close eye on Bridget, but she gives nothing away.

Your tour guide leads you from the car park, along a winding path to the tombs. The sun is climbing higher now and the desert is sweltering.

The valley is dotted with little entrances that take you down into the darkened chambers, dug centuries ago for Ramesses II, Tutankhamun and many of Egypt's kings. The tomb of Seti I takes you deep underground. It's a disorientating maze of antechambers and passageways. Despite your efforts to keep an eye on Bridget, you become separated from her and the rest of the group.

Eventually your tour guide calls out, 'Come along, Mr Banks. It's time to go.'

As you make your way out of the tomb, you imagine drinking a cool glass of orange juice when you get back to the *Sobek*. But as you approach the entrance, something rumbles above you. Thudding stones fill the tunnel and the tomb plunges into darkness.

The thought of being buried alive in a pharaoh's tomb does not appeal. You immediately reach into your satchel and pull out the box of matches. You strike one, half expecting to find a mummy lunging out of the darkness. Instead, you discover a large scarab painted on the wall.

You make your way to the end of the tunnel and find the pile of fallen stone blocks. You tap one and it feels loose. It's possible this is just a rockfall and you're the victim of unfortunate timing . . . But the tomb has stood here for thousands of years, and the chances of there being a cave-in while you're inside are almost zero, so this feels more like an attempt on your life.

To be sure, you must first find your way out.

Three of the blocks are larger than the others. Pulling one out could leave an opening that's big enough to crawl through. But you must be careful. Removing them could make the rocks above it fall down, sealing you inside.

See if you can work out which block can be removed safely to create an opening you can escape through.

If you remove:

- **Block A**, turn to **chapter 34**
- **Block B**, turn to **chapter 22**
- **Block C**, turn to **chapter 14**

33

SUSPECT MAZE CHASE

You decode the last hieroglyphic and reorder the letters in your detective's journal to find the name 'Brigadier'.

Did he really kill Clara? Or did she make a mistake in the chaos that followed the falling rock? As you turn the question over in your mind, something flashes in the corner of your eye.

You immediately look round and glimpse someone in a heavy trench coat. There's a glint of gold on their shoulder, like a button or some sort of military insignia. Whoever it is, they're hunching their shoulders as they run, in order to avoid being seen. But they aren't running for the exit like everyone else . . .

So you go after them.

The hurrying figure weaves through the towering stone columns and ducks through a little doorway at the foot of the temple's grand entrance building.

You follow them inside and find a dusty corridor that leads you into a maze of tunnels and passageways.

See if you can find your way through the maze and catch up with the suspicious person in the trench coat. But, be warned – they're quick, so you should avoid doubling back or retracing your steps, and you'll never solve the case if you don't get out safely . . .

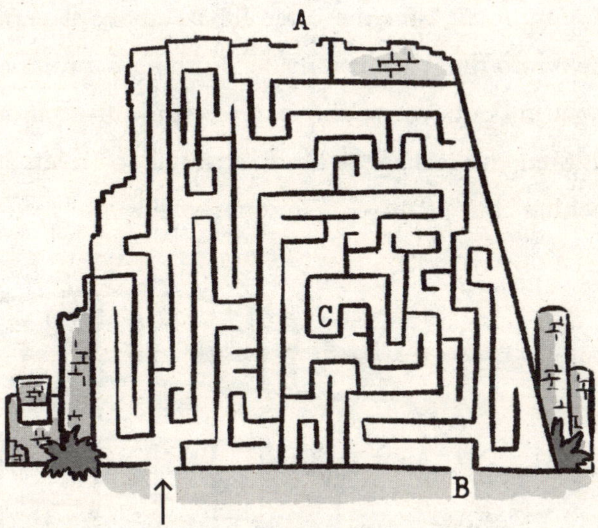

If you find your way to:

- **A**, turn to **chapter 18**
- **B**, turn to **chapter 13**
- **C**, turn to **chapter 21**

THE TYRE TRACK TEST

The block slides out and daylight floods into the tunnel . . .

A moment later the three blocks above it crash down into the space you made, crushing your hopes of getting out. You're about to scream in frustration but then you realize the blocks that fell down left an opening above that you can squeeze through.

You pull yourself out of the tomb and take a deep breath of the desert air. It might be hot and dry, but after the musty old tomb it tastes as sweet as a summer meadow. You pick yourself up and dust off your clothes.

The valley is deserted now, so you make your way back along the winding path to the car park and find that the bus you arrived in has gone.

It's hard not to take this personally. But it's also a clue that the rockfall was caused by someone who was determined to leave you behind.

The sooner you get back to the group, the more chance you have of catching the Scarab.

Looking at the dusty ground in the car park, you can make out several sets of tyre tracks. Follow the tracks and see if you can work out which set was left by the bus that brought you here so you can go after them.

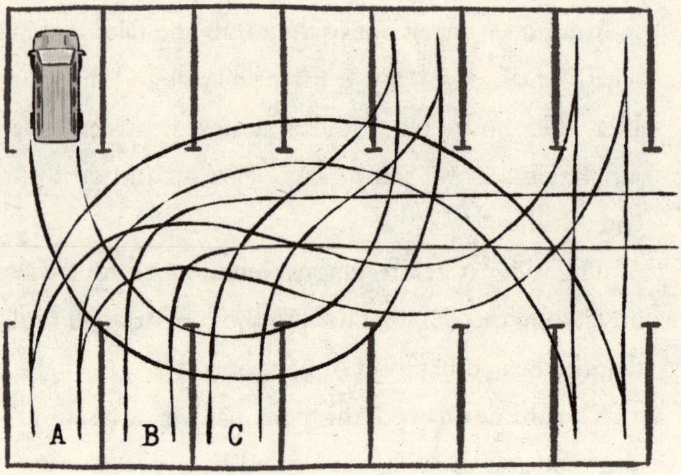

If you think you should follow tyre tracks:

- **A**, turn to **chapter 31**
- **B**, turn to **chapter 20**
- **C**, turn to **chapter 35**

TYRE TRACK OPTION C

You follow the tracks as closely as you can, but before long, you discover that they lead you to a parked truck on the other side of the car park. You shake your head in dismay.

How did this happen? you wonder.

The time you spent trapped inside the tomb must've left you dehydrated and disorientated. So you take a rest and start over.

This time, follow the tracks more carefully.

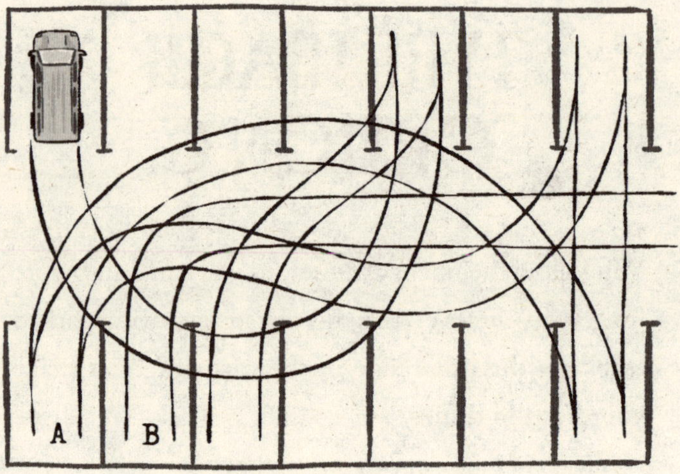

If you think you should follow tyre tracks:

- **A**, turn to **chapter 31**
- **B**, turn to **chapter 20**

36

DINNER POISONING

You stare at the four bottles you've pieced back together. Apart from a few shards, they're all intact. The bottles themselves don't reveal anything, apart from the fact that none of them are port bottles.

As you put the broken glass back in the bin, you can't deny the feeling that the Scarab is still several steps ahead of you.

The poisoned bottle of port could be anywhere by now. But as a great detective once said, 'Even the absence of any clues is a clue to something.' And that's enough to convince you that you're on the right lines.

As you try to figure out your next step, the door opens and Abasi looks in. 'Hi there,' he says, with a smile. 'Dinner's ready, if you're hungry?'

You thank him as your stomach gurgles, then look back at the bottles on the shelf behind the bar. There must be a clue here somewhere . . . But a break while you think it over might help you spot whatever you're missing, so you follow Abasi to the Dining Room.

A table in the Dining Room has been laid and everyone else is here.

'Sorry to keep you all waiting,' you say, as you sit down between Gerald and Clara, who's still visibly upset.

'It's quite all right,' the Brigadier says with a jovial smile. 'We all know you've been busy puzzling.'

'Have you found my necklace?' Lady Hamilton asks.

'Not yet,' you reply, feeling caught off-guard.

'Well then, you can't be very good at puzzling, can you?' Lady Hamilton snaps.

You're about to defend yourself when Gerald asks, 'Anyone fancy some port?' His eyes zero in on the bottle sitting in the middle of the table.

'What a good idea,' the Brigadier replies. 'Port always livens things up.'

'Yes, please,' Bridget says, raising her empty glass.

'Constance, will you do the honours?' Lady Hamilton says.

'Of course,' Constance replies.

Gerald grabs the port and with a swift twist the seal cracks open. His hand trembles as he pours himself a glassful.

'Steady on, old boy,' the Brigadier says and reaches across the table to take it from him. He offers Clara a glass but she shakes her head.

'Isn't port usually passed to the left?' Lady Hamilton remarks.

'Who cares about that?' Gerald replies. 'Get it open, I say.'

Lady Hamilton scowls.

'Quite right, your ladyship,' the Brigadier says and passes the bottle to Bridget, who's sitting on his left. She helps herself and passes it to Constance, who fills her glass and offers to pour some for Lady Hamilton. She immediately shakes her head, so Constance places the bottle back in the middle of the table.

'I don't normally drink,' Clara says, 'but you know, I think I might have one . . . for Miss Patti.'

'That's the spirit,' the Brigadier says with a smile, as she takes the bottle and pours herself a glass. You politely return the bottle to the centre of the table and the stewardess arrives to serve dinner.

Under normal circumstances, the dinner would be a lovely meal of lamb cutlets, asparagus and rice with dates and apricots. But tonight's meal is subdued by the gloomy cloud of Miss Patti's murder and the theft of Lady Hamilton's necklace. The Brigadier, Bridget, Gerald and Lady Hamilton start a conversation about tomorrow's excursion to the Great Temple of Ammon, but it soon fizzles out. There isn't much to say, so everyone focuses on eating and drinking.

Before long, the glasses of port run low. The Brigadier is first to help himself to a refill. 'There's a drop more if anyone would like it,' he says.

'Why not?' Clara replies. 'I'm rather enjoying this.'

The Brigadier smiles, but passes the bottle to his left and it begins another lap around the table. Curiously, no one tops up their glass and as soon as Gerald gets his hands on the bottle, he empties the last of it into his. 'Shall I ask for another bottle?' he suggests.

'Not for me, thank you,' the Brigadier replies. 'I've hit my limit.'

'I don't drink that horrid stuff,' Lady Hamilton scoffs and Constance shakes her head.

‘Well, I fancy another glass, but I couldn’t drink a whole bottle,’ Clara says.

‘And I think you’ve had enough for one night, dear,’ Bridget adds.

Gerald shrugs it off and takes a large swig of port.

As everyone finishes their meal, Gerald starts to cough.

You immediately pat him on the back to stop him choking.

‘Are you all right, dear?’ Bridget asks, sounding concerned.

Gerald can’t reply. He just keeps coughing and clutching his throat.

‘Leave it to me!’ the Brigadier says, coming to help, and starts thumping Gerald’s back.

You watch, along with everyone else, feeling helpless as the Brigadier hits him again and again . . . Then Gerald starts foaming at the mouth.

‘He’s been poisoned!’ you call out. ‘Just like Miss Patti!’

The Brigadier steps back and Gerald falls down dead at the table.

As the shocked horror sets in, you look at the faces of everyone round the table.

Lady Hamilton is staring at Gerald, aghast.

Constance is covering her face, recoiling in horror.

Bridget is sobbing and asking, 'How did this happen?'

The Brigadier's jaw has gone slack.

Clara is stunned. The shock of finding her colleague murdered must've drained her emotions.

How could another bottle of port poison someone? you wonder.

'Nobody move!' the Brigadier barks, like he's back in the army. He grabs a nearby napkin and covers Gerald's face.

A few minutes later Abasi arrives with his father, the Captain. The shock of what's just happened immediately writes itself across their faces. 'Please can you all return to your cabins?' the Captain says, struggling with his emotions. 'Until we know what's going on, I want you all kept safe.'

Back in your cabin you pull out your detective's journal and draw a plan of the dining table, marking out who was sitting where, and draw the port bottle in the centre.

Your thoughts immediately begin to turn over . . .

Anyone who drank from the bottle *after* the poison was added would've suffered the same fate as Gerald. So cast your mind back to dinner, then take your pen and retrace the route the port bottle took around the table. Whoever the evidence points to could be the Scarab and will be worth keeping a close eye on during tomorrow's excursion to the temple.

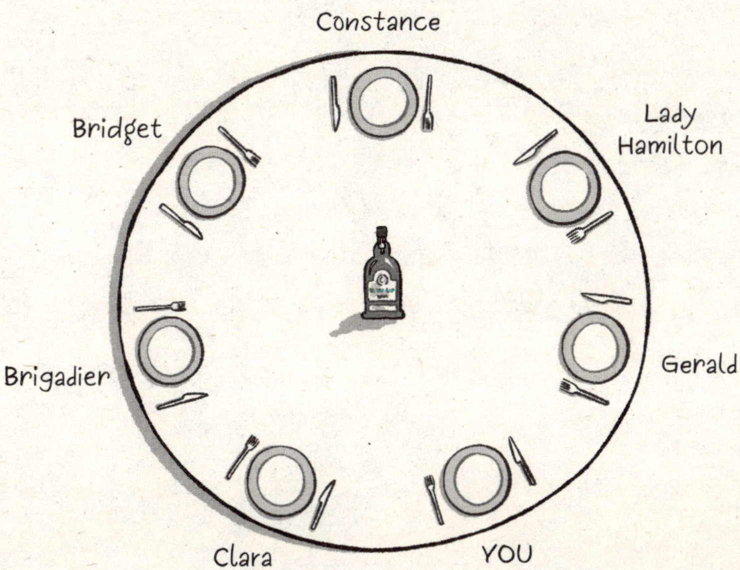

If you find it implicates more than one person, go with your instincts, follow whoever you think it might be and keep an eye out for any other clues.

If you decide to follow:

- **The Brigadier**, turn to **chapter 24**
- **Clara**, turn to **chapter 19**
- **Lady Hamilton**, turn to **chapter 16**
- **Constance**, turn to **chapter 9**
- **Bridget**, turn to **chapter 28**

37

SHOPPING IN THE BAZAAR

'You know what, I know someone back home who would love a papyrus postcard,' you say, thinking of the Professor.

'Then you're in the right place,' the man says, and rotates a rack, revealing stacks of postcards. Each one is hand-painted with beautiful Egyptian hieroglyphics and ancient gods. Before you realize it, you have selected enough to fill an entire scrapbook.

'Thank you, sir,' he says as you hand over your money without bargaining.

'Thank you for rescuing me,' you say.

The man frowns, looking confused.

'I was looking for the bus I arrived in, but my friends left without me,' you explain.

'Ah! Let me help you,' he says, and leads you outside to a little courtyard where two camels are kneeling on the ground.

'Climb on,' he says and helps you up. 'I'll take you to your friends.'

‘Are you sure? Our boat is moored near the Temple of Ammon.’

‘Sure, it’s no problem,’ he says, and hands you a parasol to protect you from the sun.

‘Thank you so much!’ you say, and together you form a short camel train and set off across the desert dunes.

The sun beats down, but the swaying motion of your camel lulls you into an oasis of calm as you wander up and down the dusty dunes. This is an experience like nothing else.

Before long, you leave the dunes and enter the outskirts of Luxor. Seeing civilization again is both reassuring and disappointing because it means your journey is coming to an end.

Soon the Temple of Ammon is towering over the city and you arrive at the jetty where the *Sobek* is moored. You climb down from your camel and thank the man. As you pay him for his help, he bows gratefully.

As you walk up the gang-ramp, your thoughts return to catching the Scarab.

Turn to **chapter 23**

38

DON'T BUY FROM THE SHOP

'I'm fine, thanks,' you tell the man. 'I just want to find my friends. We have a boat moored by the Temple of Ammon. Do you have a car or anything that I can ride in?'

'Me? Oh-no. I'm not a rich man,' he says, laughing. 'But I can help you.' He beckons you to follow him out through the back of his shop. Outside is a little courtyard with two camels sitting on their knees.

'Camels have been crossing the desert for thousands of years,' he says as he unties one of them. 'Here, climb on,' he continues, showing you how.

'Really?' you ask, a little unsure about riding a camel.

'Oh, yes. Head east until you reach the Nile, then cross the river and go south, then you will find your friends,' he says.

'Thank you,' you reply.

'It's my pleasure,' he says.

You open your satchel and pull out some money.

The man's face lights up with a grateful smile. 'You want some more water?' he asks, gesturing to a stack of bottles.

They look inviting, but you shake your head. 'I'm good, thanks.'

'OK. Just head away from the sun,' he tells you.

'Thanks,' you say, settling into the saddle. The huge camel rises up. With a slap on its backside, you start out across the desert dunes, waved off by the man.

It feels like you're setting off on another adventure as your camel leads you up and over the dunes. Your imagination spirals at the thought of how many other explorers have dreamed of doing exactly this.

You head away from the sun, just as the man told you to, but hours pass and still you don't find any sign of the Nile.

The swaying motion of the camel rocks you from side to side and the beating sun sears your head and burns your shoulders through your clothes. You've never sweated so much in your life. The last dregs of water the man gave you disappeared a long time ago.

It becomes the only thing you can think about, and you wish you had bought a crate of water from the man.

You press on, but even though the sun is still following its path across the sky, you have to admit it, you're completely lost!

Gradually, extreme dehydration sets in and you don't find any sign of Luxor, or anything else. It's just sand dunes all the way to the horizon. Your vision begins to blur and your head starts to pound. You cling to your camel, which shows no signs of fatigue – they really are the ships of the desert!

Eventually you black out and fall from your camel. He stops, lingering beside you. You welcome the shade and tell yourself you'll just lie there for a minute until you feel well enough to continue.

But, before long, the camel grows tired of waiting and heads home, leaving you lying on the sand to die in the searing desert heat, wishing you had bought more water.

THE END

COBRA A

As soon as you spot the extra point sticking out from under the towel, you reach down and pull out a folded note that says:

> Arlo,
>
> Someone is hiding in your bathroom. I saw them slip into your cabin while I was helping the stewards preparethe rooms. Get out now!
>
> Abasi

You immediately feel a wave of relief – it's good to have a friend looking out for you! But that feeling is instantly quashed by the reality that someone dangerous is waiting, right there in your bathroom!

Escaping a very real danger gives you a new lease of life. You duck out of your cabin and head back to the Passenger Lounge to look again at the broken bottles.

After five minutes of studying the broken pieces, your fresh approach helps you assemble them into four bottles.

Turn to **chapter 36**

40

THE BIG REVEAL

All the conversation stops as you enter the Passenger Lounge. Bridget is standing at the bar. The Brigadier is sitting at the backgammon table with Lady Hamilton and Constance.

They all look up.

The Brigadier breaks the silence and says, 'Arlo! Nice of you to join us.'

'Thank God you're all right. I thought something terrible had happened,' Constance says.

'Constance, I've warned you about thinking,' Lady Hamilton snaps.

'I'm fine . . . luckily,' you reply, and cast a suspicious eye around the room as you approach the backgammon table. You open your satchel, take out your detective's journal and lay out all the clues and pieces of evidence you've found.

'Someone's been busy,' Bridget says, raising an inquisitive eyebrow.

'I have,' you reply. 'Here's everything I know about the Scarab.' Open-mouthed shock fills the faces of everyone in the room as they stare at you.

EVIDENCE LIST

- Clara and Miss Patti were insurance lawyers who tracked fraudsters and cheats.
- The gold crest on the envelope from their London office was also on the letter in Lady Hamilton's handbag, which you saw when she emptied her things on to the Sundeck.
- Miss Patti was poisoned by the port she drank while playing backgammon in the Passenger Lounge, but the bottle we drank from at dinner was brand new, so the poison was added while we ate.
- Miss Patti died in her cabin from the poison. The Scarab then tightened her pink neck scarf to cover their tracks, and shot her to bring everyone running to her cabin, leaving the coast clear to steal Lady Hamilton's diamond necklace.
- Gerald, however, was killed because he had an insatiable appetite for alcohol, which also made him, at times, outspoken.
- Clara only drank one glass, not one drop more, so the port passed from her to Gerald without her drinking any.

- In addition, when Clara became another victim, I realized the Scarab couldn't be her and was someone else.
- The stab wound Clara received was short and thin, but it was deep enough to kill her.

Even the usually spiteful Lady Hamilton is silent.

'Now, these clues don't tell us everything,' you continue. 'But a number of other clues I've found have led me to the conclusion that the person who took Lady Hamilton's diamond necklace, and murdered Miss Patti, Gerald and Clara is . . .'

If you think it was:

- **The Brigadier**, turn to **chapter 41**
- **Bridget**, turn to **chapter 42**
- **Lady Hamilton**, turn to **chapter 43**
- **Constance**, turn to **chapter 44**

41

IT WAS THE BRIGADIER

You point to the trench coat you found in the maze of tunnels at the temple.

'All the evidence points to a murderer who knew how long the poison would take to kill Miss Patti, and that a gunshot would draw us all to her cabin, leaving the coast clear for them to steal the necklace,' you say. 'It was perfect. You could say it was planned with military precision . . . Brigadier?' The moment your eyes rest on the Brigadier he glares at you.

'You surely can't be accusing me of murder?' he barks.

'Why not?' you reply. 'You've killed before, haven't you? In the trenches?'

'That was a war!' he snaps.

'Murder is murder,' you say.

'If that's your point of view, fine,' he says with an air of indignance. 'But why on earth would I steal a diamond necklace? Everyone here knows my military pension is more than generous!' He bangs his fist on the table, making your detective's journal jump. 'I suggest you go back through your list and think again!'

As soon as you start looking at the evidence and clues, you realize the Brigadier is right. There must be something you missed the first time.

EVIDENCE LIST

- Clara and Miss Patti were insurance lawyers who tracked fraudsters and cheats.
- The gold crest on the envelope from their London office was also on the letter in Lady Hamilton's handbag, which you saw when she emptied her things on to the Sundeck.
- Miss Patti was poisoned by the port she drank while playing backgammon in the Passenger Lounge, but the bottle we drank from at dinner was brand new, so the poison was added while we ate.
- Miss Patti died in her cabin from the poison. The Scarab then tightened her pink neck scarf to cover their tracks, and shot her to bring everyone running to her cabin, leaving the coast clear to

steal Lady Hamilton's diamond necklace.

- Gerald, however, was killed because he had an insatiable appetite for alcohol, which also made him, at times, outspoken.
- Clara only drank one glass, not one drop more, so the port passed from her to Gerald without her drinking any.
- In addition, when Clara became another victim, I realized the Scarab couldn't be her and was someone else.
- The stab wound Clara received was short and thin, but it was deep enough to kill her.

If you think it was:

- **Bridget**, turn to **chapter 42**
- **Lady Hamilton**, turn to **chapter 43**
- **Constance**, turn to **chapter 44**

42

IT WAS BRIDGET

You point to the bottles standing neatly on the shelf behind the bar. 'All the evidence points to a murder committed by someone who knew that Gerald liked to drink. Anyone could tell that much from the blotches on his face.'

'And the glass in his hand!' Lady Hamilton adds with a snort.

'Quite,' you say. 'So it made perfect sense for someone to poison the port. Unfortunately, on the first evening Gerald opted for wine instead, leaving Miss Patti to take the poison. Isn't that right, Bridget?'

Bridget recoils in fury as your accusation hits home.

'How dare you?' she says. 'I loved Gerald! Despite his faults.' She stares at you with an indignant glare. 'And even if I had wanted to kill my husband, I certainly wouldn't have started by poisoning and shooting a lawyer just to steal some diamond necklace. Or, more to the point, killing their partner once my husband was dead!'

'Are you quite sure about this accusation?' the Brigadier asks you. 'I mean, your reputation suggests you're quite the puzzler, but all I can see here is a lot of silly guesswork.'

'Absolutely, Brigadier,' Lady Hamilton says, and waves her fan at the stewardess to order another round of drinks. 'It's enough to make me think he's the culprit!'

The embarrassing failure of your accusation compels you to join the others in a glass of orange juice. Sadly, the killing spree isn't over yet. A few short minutes later the Brigadier and Bridget start foaming at the mouth. You get up to help them, but an agonizing pain fills your gut and you collapse on the floor. As the others slump in their chairs, the last thing you see is Lady Hamilton and Constance discreetly getting up.

'I think we'd better pack our things,' Lady Hamilton says, as she removes the Brigadier's wallet fromhis pocket.

'I quite agree, Martha,' Constance replies, as she strips Bridget of her watch and checks the time. 'The next train to Cairo leaves in forty minutes.'

THE END

43

IT WAS LADY HAMILTON

You look up from your detective's journal. 'It all points to someone with a ruthless determination,' you say. 'Possibly even someone with nothing left to lose. Isn't that right, Lady Hamilton?'

'I'm sorry? Are you accusing me of multiple murders?' she says, laughing, and she flaps her fan to dismiss the accusation.

Burning embarrassment floods your face, but Lady Hamilton isn't finished. 'How on earth am I supposed to have shot Miss Patti in her cabin *and* stolen my own diamond necklace while I was swimming?' she asks. 'Honestly, this is just ridiculous.'

'I couldn't agree more, Lady Hamilton,' the Brigadier says, and pours her another drink.

'Quite right,' Constance chips in.

Lady Hamilton sits up. 'I don't think you can call this an *investigation*,' she says. 'You should hand your evidence over to the police, at once. Let the authorities deal with this professionally instead of wasting time and letting someone get away with murder!'

The weight of awkward embarrassment leaves you lost for words, and the five of you sit there until Abasi brings in the police from the temple. They accept the evidence you've collected, but are quick to point out that most of it won't stand up in court, even if it does help them work out who killed Miss Patti, Gerald and Clara.

If being humiliated weren't enough, Lady Hamilton refuses to let the police leave until they agree to search the boat for her diamond necklace – starting with your cabin.

THE END

44

IT WAS CONSTANCE

'All the evidence indicates that these murders were committed by someone who planned every detail,' you begin. 'They knew how long the poison would take to kill Miss Patti, that a gunshot would draw everyone to her cabin, and that it would give them just enough time to steal Lady Hamilton's diamond necklace *and* provide them with an alibi.' You draw a breath. 'Isn't that right, Constance?'

Your sweeping stare turns to the timid-looking lady who's spent the entire trip hiding behind newspapers and lurking in Lady Hamilton's shadow.

'I . . . don't know what you mean,' she stammers.

'Yes you do,' you reply. 'You are the Scarab, and this was your plan – to get your revenge on the lawyers who ruined Lady Hamilton. By anyone's standards, it was an audacious crime. But you couldn't do it alone . . .' Your eyes leave Constance. 'Could she, Lady Hamilton?'

The former heiress gasps. 'Whatever do you mean?'

You look her straight in the eye. 'I mean, you were the accomplice in your handmaid's plan to reverse your misfortune.'

Lady Hamilton starts frantically waving her fan, as though she's trying to dismiss your accusation. But she can't escape the truth . . .

'It's fair to say that your divorce was expensive, isn't it?' you say.

'That's putting it mildly!' she splutters. 'The lawyers *took everything*. They left me *homeless*!' She clutches Constance's hand. 'The both of us!'

'Yes. Their letter said the sale of your estate was finalized and will proceed in due course. And you sat, in that very chair, when the Brigadier was venting about losing his trench coat, and said, "I've lost enough *things* through my divorce to know that things don't *really* matter."'

'So what if I did say that?' Lady Hamilton snaps. 'Words don't make me a murderer.'

'No, but stabbing someone does,' you reply.

Lady Hamilton's jaw drops, and hers isn't the only one.

You take out the letter you found in Miss Patti's

pocket and say, 'When Miss Patti received this letter you said you got letters like that all the time. It sounded like a throwaway remark to the rest of us, but it was actually very accurate. A letter just like it was in your handbag when you emptied everything on to the Sundeck, while pretending to search for your necklace.' You point to the gold crest on the envelope. 'It's a match for the one in your handbag. And that isn't a coincidence. Miss Patti's law firm had been dealing with you for months, so they must've known how vicious you could be – anyone who's spent more than five minutes with you would know that. And I'll bet they didn't trust you an inch.'

'Even if that's true, why would we do any of this?' Lady Hamilton demands.

'Why indeed? Your initial plan was simple: travel to a distant part of the world and have your last family heirloom stolen, then return home and claim a healthy amount from the insurance firm. As soon as the dust had settled, you could sell the diamond necklace in secret, away from the beady eyes of Mortan & Flinn – the lawyers who, according to the letter Miss Patti received, were deciding the fate and sale of your family estate, stripping you of everything.

'Money always matters to the wealthy. And your plan had riches *and* revenge – it was perfect.

'But then the lawyers you must've loathed sent Clara and Patti to keep an eye on your diamond necklace. As soon as they arrived, you realized you couldn't let them discover your plan. They had to die. Luckily for you, Miss Patti's murder provided a perfect distraction – everyone saw you dripping with water instead of jewels – so all you needed to do was put on a show when you "discovered" that a thief had struck.'

You point to a bottle of port on the freshly stocked shelf behind the bar. 'At first you thought a simple poisoning would be enough to bump them off. But Clara didn't drink while she played backgammon so you were forced to kill them one at a time.

'When you tried a second time, Gerald's thirst for alcohol led him to take the hit you hid in the port.' You turn to Bridget. 'I'm so sorry.'

She gives you an appreciative smile. 'I always knew the drink would kill him.'

'Then, after Lady Hamilton so kindly gave Constance the day off,' you continue, 'we all assumed she was resting in her cabin while we were on the excursion. But you were very busy, weren't you?' You turn to Constance and hold up the Brigadier's coat. 'The stewards didn't lose this; it was taken shortly after the Brigadier came on board. And Constance used it as either a disguise or a way to throw me off the scent, while she created a distraction in the temple. She scaled the temple and pushed the block off the column, creating the chaos that gave Lady Hamilton the perfect opportunity to stick the knife in – or rather, her letter opener.'

'You think Clara was killed with *my* letter opener!' Lady Hamilton scoffs. 'Miss Patti borrowed it and never returned it.'

'Maybe she didn't,' you say. 'But that wouldn't stop someone as precise as Constance from taking it while Miss Patti lay dead on her cabin floor. As much as you say you don't care for *things*, you needed the letter opener for something else, didn't you?'

Eyes around the room narrow at you.

'Clara's wound was short and thin, but it went deep enough to kill her, eventually. In the confusion, she tried to identify the Brigadier, but all she did was fall for Constance's disguise.

'The local police have Clara's body. I'm sure that

when they check her wound against the letter opener they'll find a match. Along with traces of her blood on the blade and Lady Hamilton's fingerprints on the handle.'

Lady Hamilton shuffles in her seat but she doesn't deny the uncomfortable truth.

'You might have got away with it, too, if a champion puzzle-solver hadn't joined the trip!' the Brigadier remarks.

'Very true,' you say. 'But somewhere in Miss Patti's cabin Constance's cheap bracelet broke, and its scarab beads got everywhere. You didn't have time to gather them up, so they left a trail that led us right here.' You empty the pocket of the Brigadier's coat on to the table and out falls another bead carved with a scarab. It lands next to the bead you sealed in an evidence bag in Miss Patti's cabin. 'I'm sure the local police can get a fingerprint off this that will match yours, Constance,' you say.

Lady Hamilton jumps up from her seat and turns on Constance. 'You said this *scheme* couldn't fail!' she shrieks. 'That we'd never have to worry about money again. That I'd get my life back! Now look what you've done!'

'What I've done?' Constance yells, rising from her chair like a snake from a basket. 'We're in this together. But I won't be looking after you in jail, *Lady Hamilton*. Finally you'll have to take care of yourself!'

The Brigadier places a strong hand on each of their shoulders and orders them to 'sit down, please. You aren't going anywhere.' He turns to you. 'Well done, Arlo. You've solved the case. If there wasn't so much poison on this boat, I'd buy you a drink!'

A few short minutes later Abasi arrives with the local police. They're very glad you can help them solve this case.

The Captain orders a full search of Lady Hamilton's cabin and sure enough, the police find the missing diamond necklace at the bottom of her suitcase, along with the blood-stained letter opener and the revolver Constance used to shoot Miss Patti.

The boat feels very quiet after the police take Constance and Lady Hamilton away, so you settle down and write a letter telling the Professor all about this latest puzzling adventure.

Afterwards Abasi invites you for a game of shuffleboard on the Boardwalk. But as you line up your first shot, a steward arrives with a telegram from the British government, asking you to urgently return to England – and to bring all of your puzzle-solving skills with you . . .

Quickly now – a diplomatic jet is waiting at Luxor airport to take you to your next adventure . . .

THE HIDDEN HACKER

1

THE SECRET INTELLIGENCE SERVICE

Your jet lands at RAF Northolt where a car with blacked-out windows is waiting on the runway. The sky is grey, and after the heat of Egypt, the spring breeze rolling across the airfield feels like an arctic blast.

Your driver takes pity on you and turns up the car's heater, but you still delve into your luggage and pull on an extra jumper.

The car takes you halfway across England, to somewhere hidden away in the countryside down a warren of lanes lined with oak and birch trees. You pull up outside an unassuming brown-brick building. Drab net curtains cover the windows, hiding whatever's inside.

Your driver shows you to the main entrance. Inside, a receptionist is sitting behind a wooden desk, answering phones.

As the door closes behind you, a man in a tweed suit approaches, his shoes clicking across the polished stone floor. 'Arlo! Thank you so much for coming,' he says, and shakes your hand.

'How do you know it's me?' you ask, feeling slightly unnerved.

'We know everyone who comes here, and everything about them,' he replies with a knowing smile. 'Welcome to the Secret Intelligence Service.' He points out a faded coat of arms on the wall with the motto: *Semper Occultus*. The month or so you spent studying Latin tells you it means 'Always Secret'.

'I'm Bennet Ward, Head of Home Operations.' He covers his mouth with his hand and whispers, 'I keep an eye on our agents and operatives working around the world, as well as our enemies' spies.'

'*Spies?*' you say, looking around, feeling gobsmacked. You knew this was important, but spies and the Secret Intelligence Service are more than you imagined.

'I take it you've heard of the SAS – the Special Air Service – and the Special Boat Service?' Bennet asks as he leads you to a waiting lift. 'They're two of the elite divisions in the British Armed Forces. It's the job of the SIS to keep the country, and its people, safe from rogue states, terrorists, organized criminals – anyone who poses a threat to the country. And that involves spying.'

The lift doors close, sealing you inside.

'Everything I'm about to show you has been classified as top secret, so you're forbidden to talk about it with anyone outside the building. Do you understand?' Bennet asks.

You nod. 'Of course.'

'Good man,' he says, and smiles as the lift sets off. 'Now, we called you in because we have a rather puzzling problem you might be able to help with.'

'I'll do my best,' you reply.

'I know you will,' Bennet says, nodding. 'Your work on the Orient Express and in Egypt were outstanding.'

'How do you know about that?' you ask.

Bennet smiles. 'We make it our business to know things like that. Today's gangsters, fraudsters and murderers are tomorrow's contract killers and terrorist networks.

'But what we have here is a little trickier. This building is home to many things: decoders, transcribers and translators, listeners, equipment and communicators. And they all safeguard the country's top-secret information.' He draws a deep breath. 'Our problem is, we have a hacker – someone who's found their way in here and is stealing our most valuable and important secrets.'

'I see,' you say.

'It's a major problem,' Bennet says with a grave look. 'But it's not the only problem we have. As I mentioned, we know everyone who enters the building, and everything about them. Or at least we thought we did until two days ago, when a body appeared. We don't know who the victim is, how they came to be here or why someone killed them.'

'Really?' you gasp.

'Yes, it's a real conundrum. All we have is the body.'

'Could the body be the hacker?' you ask.

'That would be the most helpful solution.' Bennet sighs. 'But unfortunately, the hacking has continued since the body turned up.'

Your eyes open wide as you take this in.

'Quite.' Bennet nods. 'I don't mind saying, we're completely stumped. Which is why we thought you might be able to help.'

'Well, I said I'd do my best,' you reply.

Bennet pats you on the shoulder. 'Thanks. I appreciate that.'

The lift opens with a *ping!* Outside is a confined corridor. The scuffed walls look like partitions – the cheapest way to divide a huge building into this many rooms. Carpet tiles and polystyrene ceiling tiles crush every sound to a hushed silence.

Bennet stops by a door and taps a code into a keypad beside the lock. The door opens with a clunk. The room inside is long, with a heavy walnut table running down the length of it. A serious-looking woman in a navy suit is sitting at the head of the table. Her jet-black hair is tied in a tight bun and her eyes hit you with an inquisitive stare.

'Madame Silvana,' Bennet says, 'allow me to introduce Arlo Banks.'

'Welcome to the SIS,' she says, and offers you a seat at the table.

'Thanks for having me,' you reply.

'Usually I'm opposed to the idea of asking for outside help, but your record is exceptional so I'll keep an open mind for the time being,' she says, and you realize that this is some sort of test.

Bennet gives you a reassuring smile. 'So, Arlo, shall we start by following the lead we have on our hacker, or would you like to see our mysterious murder victim?'

If you would like to investigate:

- **The lead on the hacker**, turn to **chapter 3**
- **The murder victim**, turn to **chapter 5**

2

EXIT B

The air duct is a twisting tunnel of corrugated aluminium that snakes behind the ceiling tiles that cover the building. The duct leads you up and down until the tunnel doubles back on itself.

You're almost dizzy, but there's nothing you can do besides follow it.

Eventually you end up squeezing out of an opening on the roof.

You pick yourself up and brush off the dust that collected on your clothes in the tunnel. As the drizzle falls, you look around. The roof is home to a huge collection of aerials, dishes and antennas, presumably scanning the airwaves for any coded messages.

As you try to imagine how the killer might've escaped from here, an access door opens and Bennet appears. 'Did you find anything?' he asks.

You shake your head. 'No. But it was worth a look.'

He smiles. 'That's OK. Come on in, I'll explain how this place works and take you through everything we know about the hacker. I could even rustle up some tea.'

'That'd be great,' you reply, and follow him inside.

Turn to **chapter 3**

3

THE LEAD ON THE HACKER

'So, why is the hacker doing this?' you ask.

'That's a good question,' Madame Silvana says, looking impressed.

'The truth is, we have very little to go on,' Bennet replies with a shrug. 'From the pattern of their behaviour, I suspect they're one of our agents who's either gone rogue, been radicalized and switched sides, or simply decided to make some money selling our secrets to the highest bidder.'

'While we're committed to keeping the country safe, it's important to remember that not everyone feels that way,' Madame Silvana says. 'So we keep track of where everyone goes inside the building.'

Bennet flicks a switch and a projector shines a grid of numbers on the end wall behind Madame Silvana. 'This is a list of rooms where the hacker has struck and removed several pieces of top-secret information,' he says. 'Everyone who works here has a pass that allows them to access specific rooms.

The hacker must have a skeleton pass that gives them the freedom of the building,' Bennet explains. 'Before we search all these rooms, I thought your puzzle-solving skills might help us save some time. If you can spot an odd one out, it could lead us to whichever room the hacker has been using.'

2	3	5	7	11	13	17	19	23
29	31	34	37	41	43	47	53	59
61	67	71	73	79	83	89	97	101

- If you think you should investigate:
- **Room 34**, turn to **chapter 8**
- **Room 71**, turn to **chapter 11**
- **Room 101**, turn to **chapter 18**

4

LINE A

The room at the end of Line A is tucked away at the end of a corridor, behind an unassuming door. You turn the handle, and to your surprise it opens.

It's a cramped room, full of racks holding bottles of bleach, cleaning fluids, buckets and mops. You're about to turn back and find Bennet when someone asks, 'Can I help you?'

You look back inside and realize a man in overalls is sitting on a plastic chair behind one of the racks.

'Oh, sorry,' you say. 'I was just looking for something. Is there a phone in here?'

The man eyes you with suspicion. 'Who wants to know?'

'I'm Arlo Banks,' you reply, as a wave of nervousness hits you. This building is full of secrets, but only someone with something to hide would be so defensive. 'I'm, er, checking all the phone lines are connected.'

'In that case,' he says with a thoughtful expression, 'I'd better not stand in your way.' He raises a hand, directing you to a telephone screwed to a wall in the far corner.

'Thanks,' you say. As soon as you lift the receiver, you feel a pinprick in your neck. You wheel round to find the man is standing behind you. You're about to say something, but the sedative works quickly and you collapse into his waiting arms as the strength in your body drains away.

Your head begins to spin and your eyes lose their focus. The bottles of bleach merge into a haze of blue and yellow, before everything goes black.

You never wake up and your body is never found. Your disappearance becomes another secret, locked away here, along with every trace of you even entering the building.

THE END

5

THE MURDER VICTIM

Bennet leads you back along the corridor to Room 88, and pulls out a key that's connected to his belt. 'You can never be too careful,' he says, as he unlocks the door and ushers you inside.

The room is square and confined. The far wall is home to four clocks, showing the times in cities around the world.

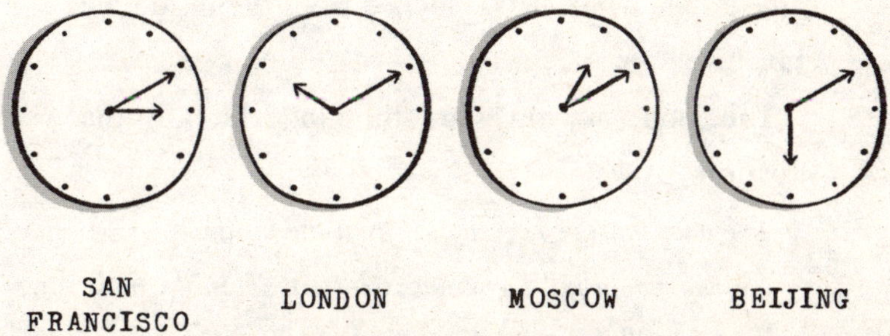

The window behind the greying net curtain is sealed shut by layers of paint that have built up over the years. Other than an air vent in the ceiling, there's nothing in here besides the body of a man lying face down on the floor. He's wearing a well-worn cream linen suit. His face is as wrinkled as the suit, and his hair is white. The handle of a large hunting knife is sticking upright out of his back.

'This really is a locked-room mystery,' Bennet says. 'It was sealed until we broke in.'

'So, you think the killer locked the door as they left?' you ask.

Bennet shakes his head and points to the doorframe. It's splintered from where a bolt has been forced open. 'No. It was locked from the inside,' he explains.

You nod, as you start thinking through the situation . . .

The door must've been bolted from the inside.

No one would kill themselves with a knife in the back.

And the killer couldn't have climbed out of the window, resealed it with layers of paint and then scaled down the brickwork!

You start searching the room, knocking on the

walls. They all sound hollow, so you conclude they must be the same partitions that divide the rest of the floor into rooms and offices. The floor, however, is solid concrete covered in carpet tiles, which leaves the ceiling . . .

You look up and find an air vent among the polystyrene tiles.

'Could the murderer have escaped through the air vent?' you ask.

'In my experience, anything is possible,' Bennet replies. 'We haven't looked at that. Would you like to?'

If you:

- **Decide to investigate the air vent**, turn to **chapter 19**
- **Return to the briefing room for more information**, turn to **chapter 3**

6

SEPTEMBER OCTOBER

You tap the code into the keyboard and the door replies with a *gleep!*

You try it again, but the same sound tells you the room is staying locked. You scratch your head and consider going back to Bennet and seeing if he has another lead.

But before you give up, you decide to look again through the keyholes to see if you can figure out another solution that will open the door.

If you think the code is:

- **Semper Occultus**, turn to **chapter 29**
- **Jumper Over Dust**, turn to **chapter 13**

7

LINE D

As soon as you spot the spur line that connects Line D to Room 34, you realize it must be a clue to something!

You turn to the nearest telephonist and say, 'Excuse me, where's Room Thirty-Four?'

She plugs in the call and looks annoyed by the interruption, then points you towards a maintenance map that shows the phone lines running around the building, and the rooms they go to.

'Thank you,' you say, and leave her to answer her phone calls.

Turn to **chapter 8**

8

ROOM 34

Room 34 is a short way along the corridor. You arrive to find the door is locked. To your surprise, it has four keyholes, but it's unlocked by a keypad.

You stare at it, feeling confused.

Then you look through one of the keyholes and see part of a phrase written on the wall inside. Look through all the keyholes and see if you can work out which phrase will unlock the door.

If you think the code is:

- **Semper Occultus**, turn to **chapter 29**
- **September October**, turn to **chapter 6**
- **Jumper Over Dust**, turn to **chapter 13**

9

THE HOT SPOT IN THE KITCHEN

You hurry upstairs to the kitchen, which is connected to the Canteen. Lunchtime is nearly over. Usually the kitchen staff would be cleaning up and beginning their preparations for the evening meal.

But not today.

Instead of gathering plates and cutlery and loading the dishwashers, you arrive to find the staff running away as the corridor outside the Canteen fills with smoke.

'*FIRE!*' someone yells and they grab your arm to pull you away from the billowing grey clouds. You yank yourself free, determined to stay with Bennet.

'Come on, we have to put it out,' Bennet says. 'If there's a bomb in there, the fire will most likely set it off before we can defuse it.'

As the fire alarm rings through the building, you and Bennet grab two fire extinguishers from the wall by the kitchen entrance. 'Aim at the base of the flames!' he yells, and kicks open the door.

The pair of you rush in and start hosing the inferno.

Before you get the fire under control, the ceiling sprinklers come on and drench the entire room in a torrent of water.

You're soaked in seconds, and so are the flames.

It comes as a huge relief. But, as the smoke clears, you realize it's just an oven fire – the kind that can happen in any industrial kitchen – and the bomb you're looking for is nowhere near here.

'At least the building's evacuated,' you say, looking round at the empty Canteen.

'That won't matter,' Bennet replies in a sombre voice, shaking his head. 'A nuclear bomb will . . .' His sentence is cut short by a deafening blast. The whole place is torn apart by a blinding flash that incinerates every cell in your body and every living creature within five miles of you.

THE END

10

MESSAGE A

'This is an order,' Bennet says as you arrange the transcription on the table.

'Yes, and it means the hacker, and whoever they work for, knows we're on to them,' Madame Silvana adds.

'So they've set a bomb to destroy the building?' you ask, struggling to believe it.

Bennet gives you a solemn nod.

'A lot of organizations threaten our country – terror groups, criminal gangs, splinter cells – so we always take something like this very seriously,' Madame Silvana explains.

'You know this building inside out,' you remind Bennet. 'Where's the best place to hide a bomb?'

Bennet thinks for a minute. Then he opens a drawer under the table and pulls out a large roll of paper. He spreads it out on the table to reveal a detailed blueprint. 'This plan shows every room, corridor and closet in the building.'

'Great,' you say. 'If we can work out where a

bomb would do the most damage, it'll narrow our search. Then all we need to do is find and defuse it before it goes off.'

You take out your detective's journal and start making notes.

'All right, here's everything we know,' Madame Silvana begins. 'The hacker operates in secret. They have a skeleton pass that gives them access to the whole building. The tape recordings we found also tell us the hacker has a line of communication running in and out of the building, which they've used to receive messages and send out the intel they've gathered. Everything we know tells us one irrefutable fact: this hacker is organized and they don't leave anything to chance.'

Bennet nods in agreement. 'OK. There are multiple ways to trigger a modern bomb,' he says. 'Sending a signal to the Telephone Exchange is ideal if you want to set off something like an incendiary device, but it would be very risky. The switchboard staff disconnect and reconnect the phone lines hundreds of times every day. A bomb with a timer or a remote switch would be far more reliable.'

'A timer is the most reliable,' Madame Silvana

says. 'Remote signals are notoriously unreliable in buildings like this. Anyone with a military background or a just standard radio will know that.'

'OK,' you say, as your eyes scan the plan. 'This building is so big, they'll need a huge bomb to destroy it. Where could they hide one that big?'

'The largest room we have is the Canteen, up on the top floor,' Bennet says. 'But if you put a bomb there, you'd only blow the roof off.'

'True,' Madame Silvana says. 'But that would be a good place to receive a remote signal.'

'There's also the Telephone Exchange,' Bennet says, pointing to a room on the floor below the Canteen. 'They could dial in a code and set off a bomb from there.'

'Maybe, but a lot of people work there,' Madame Silvana replies. 'Hiding anything there without them getting suspicious would be difficult.'

'What about this place?' you ask, pointing to a cavernous room buried beneath the building's foundations.

'That's the Bunker,' Bennet replies. 'It's where we develop the equipment our operatives and agents use when we send them on their missions.'

'There's no way you could receive a remote signal underground,' Madame Silvana says, shaking her head.

'It's so noisy down there, they took the phones out,' Bennet adds.

'OK,' you say, noting everything in your detective's journal. 'And what sort of bomb could it be?'

'To destroy a building this size you'd need either a heavy explosive, an incendiary or a gas bomb,' Bennet explains. 'The Canteen has a good gas supply, but explosives would be your best bet. An incendiary would start a fire, but the old building – everywhere apart from the Bunker – has a sprinkler system that would put it out before the building was gutted.'

You nod and make a note of it.

Madame Silvana points to the building plan. 'A gas explosion could do the job. It would destroy the partitions and supporting walls and bring down the building. Any parts of the building that did survive the blast would be condemned, too. Although some of our intelligence could be saved,' she says.

'The Bunker is made of reinforced concrete and steel,' Bennet adds. 'It's strong enough to withstand a gas explosion on the outside, and would most likely contain one.'

'The message we intercepted says, "THE WHOLE BUILDING MUST BE DESTROYED." Could they have a bigger bomb?' you ask.

'It's possible,' Madame Silvana replies with a shrug.

Your eyes scan your notes from the conversation:

Notes

- The hacker doesn't leave anything to chance.
- They have a phone line running in and out of the building.
- Triggering an incendiary device via a phone line in the Telephone Exchange is possible but risky, and a remote signal would only work near the roof.
- The Bunker could withstand a gas bomb.
- The Canteen on the top floor has a good gas supply.
- Everywhere apart from the Bunker has a sprinkler system and phone lines.
- The Hacker's orders are: THE WHOLE BUILDING MUST BE DESTROYED and explosives would be the best bet.

‘OK, so let’s use what we know to work out what sort of bomb it is, where it could be and how the hacker is planning to set it off,’ you say, drawing a grid in your journal. Now set about crossing off the clues that contradict each other, ticking the pieces of information that fit together, and use your conclusions to illuminate other details.

Work fast and use your powers of deduction to determine what sort of bomb they could be using and where it might be . . .

	A PHONE LINE	A REMOTE CONTRL	A TIMER	THE CANTEEN	THE BUNKER	THE TELEPHONE EXCHANGE
AN EXPLOSIVE						
AN INCENDIARY						
A GAS BOMB						
THE CANTEEN						
THE BUNKER						
THE TELEPHONE EXCHANGE						

Now draw your conclusions:

The Hacker has set ____________________

in the ______________________________

triggered by a ________________________

If you think the bomb is:

- **An explosive in the Bunker triggered by a timer**, turn to **chapter 27**
- **A gas bomb in the Canteen triggered by a phone line**, turn to **chapter 36**
- **An incendiary in the Telephone Exchange triggered by a remote control**, turn to **chapter 12**

11

ROOM 71

'I think we should investigate Room Seventy-One,' you say.

Madame Silvana nods. 'OK. It's as likely as anywhere. Good luck, Arlo.'

'Thanks,' you reply.

Bennet gets up to go with you.

'Er, Bennet, can you stay here please?' Madame Silvana says. 'I need to update you on a situation in Turkey.'

'Of course,' Bennet says with a nod, and gives you directions to Room 71.

You find Room 71 without any trouble and knock on the door.

'It's open,' a voice calls out and you go in.

A small, bald man is sitting at a desk with his back to the window. The sunlight filtering through the net curtains is so strong, he's almost a silhouette. He offers you a seat and asks, 'What do you need?'

A confused expression crosses your face.

'Forgive my abruptness,' the small man says. 'People usually visit me because they want something, so I don't really do small talk.'

'Of course,' you say, nodding. But you can't help wondering, *Is this man the agent who's gone rogue and switched sides?* 'I'm looking for a secret document someone might've left in here,' you say, thinking on your feet, but you stumble and your suspicions slip out.

'I see,' the man says, and a dark cloud cuts off the sunlight, revealing his face has a grave expression. 'Well, I can assure you there are no secrets here. Only bullets.'

With a flick of his arm, he pulls a gun from under the desk and – *BANG!*

THE END

THE TELEPHONE EXCHANGE FIRE

The sound of ringing telephones fills your ears as you arrive at the Telephone Exchange. The telephonists are all busily answering and connecting calls to phone lines around the building.

The far end of the room is also home to a collection of desks where a team of women are hammering away at typewriters.

'They type up letters, transcriptions and decoded messages sent in from our agents and operatives working around the world,' Bennet explains.

'OK. We need everyone to clear the room,' Madame Silvana calls out. No one hears her over the incessant sound of typing and ringing phones.

'This'll get them out,' you say, and stride over to a red box on the wall.

You're about to set off the fire alarm when Bennet raises his hand and shouts, 'Arlo, *STOP!*'

He's found something lying in a wire tray on the

desk in the typing pool. You hurry over to see what it is.

'It's a message for the hacker,' Bennet says, and points to a transcription:

THE DEVICE YOU'RE LOOKING FOR IS WITH THE UTENSILS, GADGETS AND TOOLS.

'Maybe it's a clue to where the bomb is,' you say.

Look back over the clues you checked off in your grid and see if this clue gives you another location to investigate . . .

If you think the bomb is:

- **An explosive in the Bunker**, turn to **chapter 27**
- **A gas bomb in the Canteen**, turn to **chapter 36**

13

JUMPER OVER DUST

As soon as you press enter, the deadlocks in the door slam home with a *THUD!* and an alarm rings through the building.

Twenty minutes later you're sitting across the walnut table from a furious Madame Silvana.

'I'm telling you, that's what happened,' you protest.

'Arlo,' Bennet says, taking a lighter tone. 'We're losing vital pieces of highly confidential intelligence that help us keep the country safe, and you're typing *silly* words like *Jumper Over Dust* into door locks in the hope they'll open.'

'I know it sounds stupid,' you say, 'but I looked through the keyholes and that's what I saw, so I typed it into the keypad. It's not my fault the door didn't open.'

'Yes, you're right, Arlo,' Madame Silvana says, suddenly sounding much calmer. 'I had my doubts about recruiting you and it appears they've been proved right. This is our problem, so we'll solve it.

Thank you for coming. Bennet, please make sure Arlo gets home safely.'

And with that, your puzzle-solving days are over

THE END

14

THE SECURITY BOXES

You frantically do the sums, adding the numbers until you come up with a figure. You're not sure it's right, but under this pressure, you'll say anything.

You call out the number and the young lad rips into the security box with the crowbar.

'Are we happy?' the wrestler man asks as the Boss looks through the contents.

'Nah! Add them up again!' shouts the Boss.

You try again. And this time you get another answer.

The young lad opens the next security box, but this isn't the one they're looking for either.

After a couple more attempts the Boss has run out of patience. 'Right. Open them all up,' he orders the young lad, and turns on you. He's sweating and seething with menace. 'And when we're done, we're gonna open you up!'

THE END

15

EXPLORING ROOM 88

You look around the room and take out your detective's journal. You open it on a blank page and draw a quick sketch of the square room, noting down the position of the door, how it opens, the four clocks on the end wall and the position of the body on the floor.

'Let's compare this to the building plan,' you say. 'It might reveal something we're not seeing.'

'Sure,' Bennet says, intrigued, and unravels the plan you pored over in the Board Room. All the rooms are there, divided by their partition walls. There's also the lift and the stairs, along with the confined corridor that links everything.

You quickly find Room 88 and mark it with a star. But as you study the floorplan, something about it strikes you as odd. 'How accurate is this plan?' you ask.

'It was drawn up a few years ago, when they added the Bunker,' Bennet replies, peering over your shoulder. 'But that's the only thing that's changed. Everything else should be spot on.'

It's intriguing . . . Can you see a difference between the sketch and the building plan?

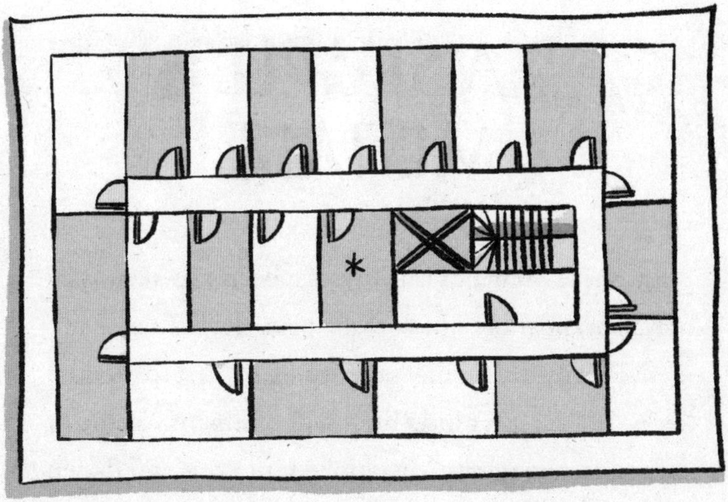

If you think there's:

- **Nothing unusual about the floorplan**, turn to **chapter 16**
- **A discrepancy between the floorplan and your sketch**, turn to **chapter 33**

16

A SIMPLE MISTAKE

You shake your head. 'I must've been mistaken,' you say, 'but the more I look at the plan, the less sure I am.'

'That's OK,' Bennet says, trying his best to reassure you. But he can't hide his disappointment. 'Some of our smartest agents have looked into this and drawn a blank. Never mind.'

As his sentence finishes, you hear a whirring sound emanating from the end wall. You both turn and stare at it, wide-eyed, watching as the end wall rises up into the ceiling, revealing someone who wants you dead . . .

THE END

17

EXIT C

Bit by bit, you crawl along the air duct. So much dust has collected in here that you soon realize the killer can't have escaped this way without leaving a trail. The duct is too tight for you to turn round, so there's no way back.

The twisting tunnel takes you all the way to the far end of the building, where you reach an air vent over the internal Telephone Exchange where calls are connected to rooms all over the building. Phones are ringing and dozens of people are answering them with all sorts of random-sounding greetings.

'Good morning, Greene Pharmaceuticals.'

'Sun Streak Travel – the holidays of a lifetime.'

'Hawks and Foster Accounting. How may I help you?'

You know very well that this building is home to none of these companies. The telephonists must be pretending to represent them for something top-secret.

Since you can't go back, there's only one thing

for it. You push the air vent out and it hits the floor with a clatter. Telephonists across the room look up from their switchboards.

There's no ladder here, so you have no choice but to jump down. Everyone stares at you, open-mouthed with disbelief. Even the women in the typing pool are gawping.

'Just trying to solve a murder,' you say with a jovial salute. Jaws drop and there's a moment of stunned silence until the phones start ringing, and they get back to work.

You dust off your clothes and look around, trying to get your bearings. You know you need to head back and find Bennet.

But then you notice an unmanned switchboard. It's a grid of sockets with wires plugged in with jack-plugs, connecting callers with phones all over the building. You watch as the calls come in to see how it all works. The telephonists answer the phones and ask the callers who they want to speak to. Then they connect the phone line with one of the extensions, and somewhere in the building the right phone starts ringing.

Every room in the building is listed next to the

sockets where the jacks plug in. But not all the lines are connected. As you watch the room, something occurs to you: if the hacker could plug an extra extension into the switchboard, they could listen into the phone calls and gather top-secret information.

The top row of jacks are where the phone lines are connected to the switchboard. From there, they plug into extensions all over the building. Follow each of the lines and see if you can find any that split off to more than one extension. If they do, they could lead you to a room where the hacker has been busy, listening to phone calls and gathering intelligence.

➡

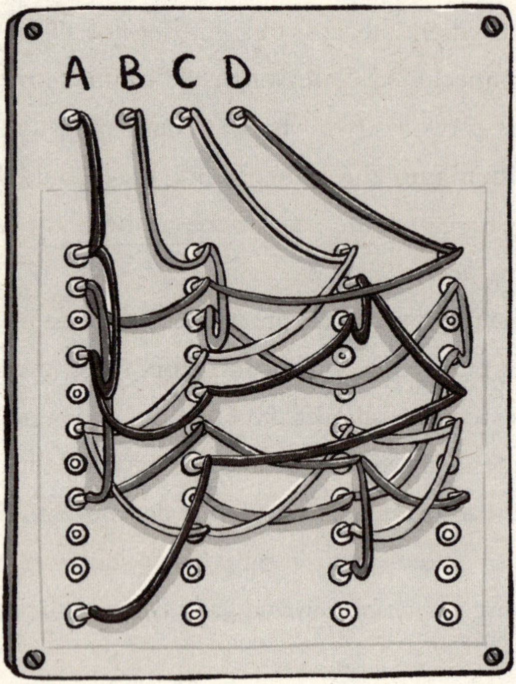

If you want to investigate the room at the end of:

- **Line A**, turn to **chapter 4**
- **Line B**, turn to **chapter 22**
- **Line C**, turn to **chapter 38**
- **Line D**, turn to **chapter 7**

18

ROOM 101

'Let's try Room 101,' you suggest.

'Are you certain?' Madame Silvana asks. Her eyes narrow and doubts creep into your mind, like an army of ants scurrying to their nest.

'Arlo, we're trying to save time, not waste it,' Bennet says. 'Try looking for a pattern or some sort of rule that doesn't rely on guesswork.'

You nod. 'OK. Let me look at the numbers again, just to double check.'

2	3	5	7	11	13	17	19	23
29	31	34	37	41	43	47	53	59
61	67	71	73	79	83	89	97	101

If you think you should investigate:

- **Room 34**, turn to **chapter 8**
- **Room 71**, turn to **chapter 11**

19

THE AIR DUCT MAZE

'You'll need a ladder,' Bennet says, and ducks out of the room.

A few minutes later he returns with a stepladder and positions it under the air vent. It's a rickety old wooden thing, covered in paint drips the same colour as the window frames.

Bennet holds it steady as you climb up.

The air vent comes away without any trouble.

'That was easy,' Bennet remarks.

'Yes, so it's possible the killer climbed into the vent and pulled it back in place before they escaped,' you say.

'So long as they had a way of getting up there,' Bennet says with an air of scepticism.

'There's only one way to find out,' you reply, and climb up into the duct.

Since you're small, you can crawl into the duct. To your surprise, you discover a maze of air ducts spanning across the floor of the building, giving the killer a potential escape route. Follow the air ducts and see if you can find any evidence that they went this way. But be careful, you don't want to get trapped . . .

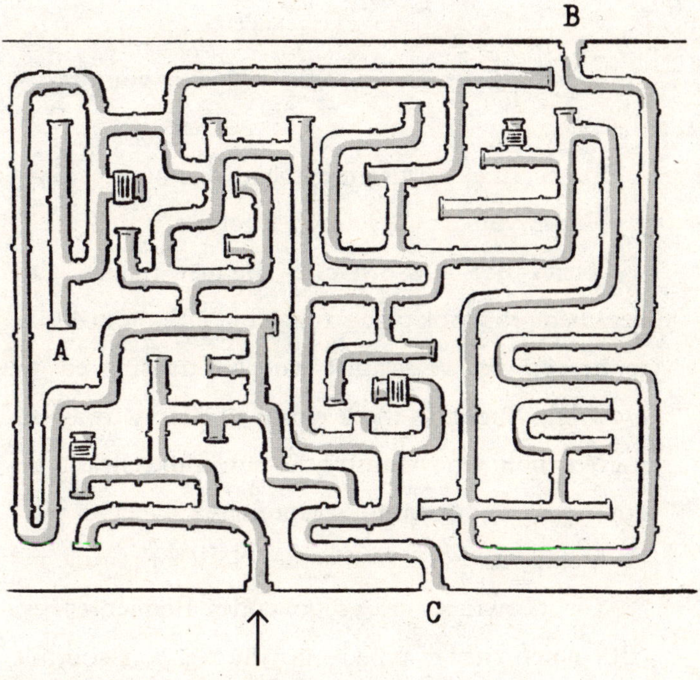

If you find your way to:

- **Exit A**, turn to **chapter 25**
- **Exit B**, turn to **chapter 2**
- **Exit C**, turn to **chapter 17**

20

THE BRIEFCASE HAS MOVED

'Why's the briefcase moved?' you ask, pointing at the photo.

Bennet's face turns grey. 'That's serious.'

'Why?' you ask. 'It's only a briefcase.'

'That's not *any* briefcase,' Bennet replies. 'It's designed to look like one, but it's actually a reinforced-steel case that can be transported to Downing Street. In the event of an enemy invasion, it gives the Prime Minister the power to unleash the country's most powerful weapons.'

A chill rushes up your spine. 'So what's inside it?'

'On its own, it's just a set of codes,' Bennet replies. 'But when they're typed into the weapon controls they'll launch a nuclear warhead. The fact it's been moved tells us the hacker is intending to set off a bomb that will destroy this entire building and everything within five miles of here. This is far more serious than I thought.' Bennet checks his watch.

'Arlo, we should order an evacuation. Get everyone as far away as possible.'

'Can we stop it?' you ask, almost too scared to hear the answer.

'There's a chance,' Bennet says. 'But only if we can figure out where they've put the bomb. Come on, we'd better move.'

The pair of you hurry back along the corridor and up the stairs to a room on the ground floor. It's full of TV screens showing corridors and doorways from around the building.

'This is the Surveillance Suite,' Bennet explains. 'Most of the time we keep it secret, because it keeps an eye on the building – spies don't like being spied on.

'This screen is a live feed from a thermal imaging camera,' Bennet says, pointing to a screen showing the outside of the building. You stare at the screen, struggling to believe what you're seeing. But now isn't the time to marvel and be impressed. A bird flies across the dark grey sky. Its wings are black but its body appears to be light grey.

'That's a regular crow,' Bennet says. 'The thermal imaging camera shows us the heat of its body.

Now, a nuclear bomb will also have a heat signature we can trace before it goes off. This camera will show it as a hot spot, giving us a chance to find it and disarm it.'

The flickering screen highlights several hot spots around the building. 'Mostly they're computers and other bits of equipment,' Bennet explains.

The largest is up in the kitchen next to the Canteen, but there's another smaller glow down in the basement.

If you think you should investigate the hot spot in:

- **The basement,** turn to **chapter 24**
- **The kitchen**, turn to **chapter 9**

21

LONDON TIME

You reach up and take down the clock that's showing London time. It's held up by a simple hook and the mechanism in the back is nothing out of the ordinary.

'Guess it's just a clock,' Bennet says, looking over your shoulder.

'Yeah, I guess so,' you say and hang it back up. 'If there is something up with these clocks, then it must be another one.'

You both step back from the wall and look again at the other clocks . . .

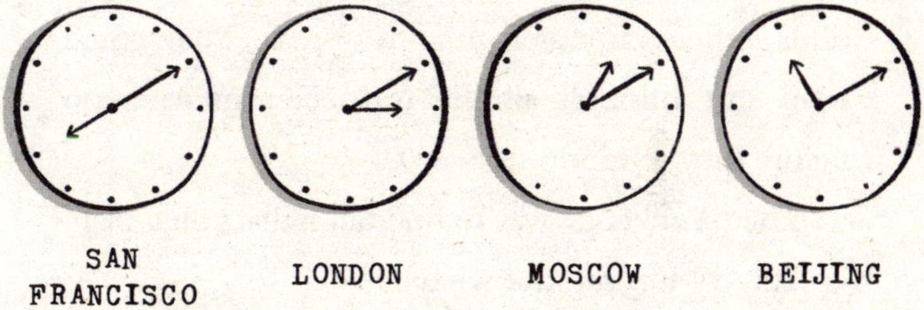

If you decide to investigate the clock for:

- **San Francisco**, turn to **chapter 41**
- **Moscow**, turn to **chapter 39**
- **Beijing**, turn to **chapter 35**

22

LINE B

Your journey to the room at the end of Line B takes you all the way down to the sub-basement, under the foundations of the building. The entrance is at the end of a long concrete tunnel. The floor feels rough under your shoes, like it was bored into solid rock.

At the end of the corridor is a large round door with a wheel on the front. You immediately recognize it as a vault and wonder, *What's inside?*

Your best guess is that the hacker has been sending intel down here. You stare at the reinforced-steel door – there's no safer place to store it. They could even sort through all the top-secret information before they send it out.

There's only one way to find out if that's their plan.

You try turning the wheel.

Unsurprisingly, it's locked. So you go and find Bennet to see if he can get you inside.

Twenty minutes later the two of you return. 'This is highly irregular,' Bennet says as he finds the right key. 'But if you're right, and the hacker has been gathering intel in here from the switchboard, then you'll have proved to be most helpful.'

With a twist of the key, the lock clicks. Bennet turns the wheel and the huge door swings open.

The vault is lined with hundreds of security boxes. Some are larger, some are smaller. A few are the size of cubbyholes. And they're all numbered.

In the centre of the room is a steel desk and a chair. Sitting on the table is a black telephone. The phone line leads to a socket in the wall.

'Looks like you were right,' Bennet says, sounding impressed. 'Someone has been sitting here, listening to phone calls.'

You pick up the phone. To your surprise, the line is dead. As you go to replace it, a huge explosion rips through the side wall. Steel deposit boxes and chunks of concrete fly at you with the force of cannonballs. You duck under the steel desk and it takes the brunt of the force.

Bennet isn't so lucky. One of the blocks knocks him unconscious.

Dust clouds circle and swirl around you, and three men in masks and yellow overalls step through the hole in the wall.

The men are dirty and sweating, like they've been hard at work for a long time. The first man into the vault pulls down his mask to reveal a grizzled face. He digs a crumpled piece of paper out of his pocket. 'Right. Where are we?' he murmurs as he unfolds it. But whatever's on the paper makes him frown and scratch his head.

'What you doing with that?' a man the size of a wrestler asks a younger-looking lad carrying a pneumatic drill.

'I thought we might need it,' the young lad replies.

The wrestler man shakes his head in dismay. 'Would you use a bulldozer to open a box of matches?'

The young lad just gawps at him.

'Look around you, son. We're in the vault. Put that back and grab the crowbar.'

As the young lad ducks back through the hole in the wall, the wrestler man says, 'Honestly, Boss. I'm amazed he can find his way out of bed in the morning!'

'He might be simple,' the Boss replies, 'but I can't make head or tail of this.'

'Jesus!' the wrestler man says as he looks at the piece of paper. 'We're gonna be here all day!'

''Ere, Boss, who's that?' the young lad says as he returns with a crowbar. You look up and realize he's spotted you!

The wrestler man grabs you and throws you against the table, pinning you down.

'What's a kid doing here?' demands the Boss.

'I'm trying to solve a murder,' you explain.

'Oh yeah?' the Boss says, frowning with disbelief.

'Yeah, my name's Arlo Banks.'

'The puzzle-solver?' the young lad interrupts. 'He was on the news!' he adds as the others stare at him.

You can't deny it – thieves can always spot a liar – but you don't know what to say.

An idea occurs to the Boss and he points to Bennet lying on the floor. 'All right, if you solve our little puzzle, we'll let you go and get some help for your friend here.'

'Sure,' you reply, nodding.

'Good lad,' the Boss says and smiles as he lightly slaps your face. 'But don't hang around. Your friend doesn't look too clever.'

They let you get up and the Boss hands you the piece of paper.

Drawn on it is a grid filled with what look like random numbers.

You stare at it, feeling as confused as the Boss was. 'Are you hackers?' you ask, desperate for a clue.

'Do we look that sophisticated to you?' the wrestler man asks.

'We're what you might call straight-down-the-line villains. Bank jobs, jewellers, that sort of thing,' the Boss explains. 'This is a special job. We're after something inside one of these boxes.

'As I'm sure you know, this place is top secret – full of codes and whatnot. I was told these numbers are some sort of special code, and the missing ones are supposed to add up to the number of the security box we're after.

'Now come on then, chop-chop. Pop your thinking cap on.'

You wrack your brains and start working out the missing numbers, before adding them together to find the answer . . .

If you think the answer is:

- **7183**, turn to **chapter 14**
- **7184**, turn to **chapter 32**

	8	27	64
125	216		512
729	1000	1331	1728
2195		3375	

23

THE ULTRAVIOLET TEST

'Our analysts down in the Bunker have an ultraviolet light,' Bennet says.

'Let's go there, then,' you say.

Ten minutes later you and Bennet are back in the Bunker. One of the analysts kindly brings you an ultraviolet torch.

'We call this a black light,' Bennet explains. 'It can be used for all kinds of things and will reveal everything from the dandruff on your shoulders to the original sketch behind the *Mona Lisa*.'

'Great,' you say. 'Let's see what it reveals about this letter.'

Bennet switches on the torch and points it at the notepaper.

Nothing appears.

'That's odd,' Bennet says, and gives the torch a slap with his hand. But it's working fine.

You turn over the notepaper and shine the light

on the other side. But still there's nothing.

'Is this a joke?' you ask.

'I don't know,' Bennet says. 'Whatever it is, we've drawn a blank.'

You were so convinced, but as Bennet switches off the torch an overwhelming sense of disappointment engulfs you.

'It's OK.' Bennet smiles. 'I think saving the building from a nuclear warhead is enough heroics for one day. Thank you so much for your help, Arlo. The country owes you a huge debt. It's just a shame the Official Secrets Act will prevent you from ever telling anyone about it.'

THE END

24

THE HOT SPOT IN THE BASEMENT

'That's a huge hot spot,' Bennet says, pointing to the kitchen at the top of the building.

'I know, and this is a big bomb,' you reply. 'But if it was producing that much heat, wouldn't that mean it had already blown up?'

Bennet nods. 'Probably.'

'Let's investigate the smaller hot spot first,' you suggest. 'If it proves to be nothing, we can check the other one.'

'That isn't nothing,' Bennet says as he opens the door to the basement room. It's a small meeting room lined with soundproofing panels. It's the kind of room where the most closely guarded secrets are discussed.

Sitting on the table is a large cone.

'That looks like the tip of a space rocket,' you remark.

'That's because it usually sits on the tip of an

intercontinental missile,' Bennet explains. 'These things are designed to be fired at enemy countries, not set off in the headquarters of the government's Secret Intelligence Service.'

You watch as Bennet carefully opens a panel in the side of the warhead. Concealed underneath it is an input keyboard and a small monitor showing a timer counting down . . .

You've never seen anything like this before – it's like something from the future – and it makes your breath freeze in your lungs.

'OK,' you say after a moment. 'So how can we stop this thing from blowing us to dust?'

Lying on the table are two pieces of paper. 'These are the launch codes,' Bennet says, scratching his head. 'Usually they're labelled, so you know which one triggers the bomb and which defuses it.'

01000100 - 01000101 - 01110100 - 01001111
- 01001110 - 01000001 - 01110100 - 01000101

01000100 - 01000101 - 01000110
- 01010101 - 01010010 - 01000101

‘The hacker must’ve torn off the labels to stop anyone deactivating the bomb,’ Bennet says and lets out a sigh.

‘It’s OK,’ you say. As the ones and zeros circle in your eyes, something occurs to you. ‘Ones and zeros are the language of binary computers!’ You open your detective’s journal. In a few seconds you’ve found a binary code sheet that translates the numbers into the alphabet. ‘If we’re quick, maybe we can use this to decode them!’

A 01000001	N 01001110
B 01000010	O 01001111
C 01000011	P 01010000
D 01000100	Q 01010001
E 01000101	R 01110010
F 01000110	S 01110011
G 01000111	T 01110100
H 01001000	U 01010101
I 01001001	V 01010110
J 01001011	W 01010111
K 01001011	X 01011000
L 01001100	Y 01011001
M 01001101	Z 01011010

If you decide to try:

01000100 - 01000101 - 01000110
- 01010101 - 01010010 - 01000101

turn to **chapter 37**

01000100 - 01000101 - 01110100 - 01001111
- 01001110 - 01000001 - 01110100 - 01000101

turn to **chapter 34**

25

EXIT A

You crawl through the air duct's twists and turns. It splits and branches off and seems to cover the entire floor of the building. The dust that's built up in there catches in your throat and makes you sneeze. You press on, looking for any sign the killer escaped this way.

But there's nothing.

You feel like giving up, but you can't remember your way back to where you started. You try to turn round, but the tunnel is too tight, so you start crawling backwards.

A few minutes later you realize you're trapped.

You call out for help, but you have no idea if anyone can hear you. Feeling tired and hoarse, you lie down.

Before long, a torrent of icy air rushes up the tunnel, set off by a thermostat somewhere in the building. As the staff in the office try to cool off, your temperature drops. You start shivering and your teeth chatter. But it's no good. You're freezing.

A few long minutes later you're overwhelmed by a wave of intense heat.

Oh thank God, you think.

But it's a mistake. You're not saved – you're suffering from hypothermia, and an unfortunate flaw in the human body makes you mistake extreme cold for warmth.

You can't help it. You relax and wriggle out of the extra jumper you put on during the drive here.

Three weeks later, after receiving several complaints about the air conditioning not working, engineers find your body. And your death becomes another secret hidden within the building.

THE END

26

DO ABSOLUTELY NOTHING

'It's fine,' you say, smiling at Bennet's worried expression, and you point to the hand grenade. 'It's still got the pin in it.'

Bennet's look of worry turns to confusion as a motor somewhere in the room starts whirring.

You both look round and realize the wall with the clocks is slowly retracting into the ceiling.

Bennet instinctively backs away, but you stand your ground.

The wall rises, revealing a darkened recess. There's a desk with a computer, a bed, a sink and even a stove – all the things the hacker has needed to stay hidden away while they ran their operation.

As your eyes take in the sight, a figure steps out of a shadowy corner, armed with a gun.

'Arlo!' Bennet shouts, trying to warn you.

But it's no use. The game is over. Either the hacker will win or you'll all lose.

The hacker knows this too.

A victorious smile stretches across his face. Then you pull the hand grenade out from behind the clock.

The hacker's eyes widen with horror as he realizes your plan. He tries to point the gun at you, but it's too late.

You've already pulled the pin out of the hand grenade.

It's a brave move, one that's worthy of any chapter in the history of the SIS. It's just a shame no one will ever know what you did.

THE END

27

THE BOMB IN THE BUNKER

Bennet leads you along the corridor, down two flights of stairs and along another corridor that takes you away from the main building. 'We call this part of the building the Bunker,' he explains.

'Then it's a good place to store intel,' you reply.

You come to a reinforced door and Bennet taps a code into a keypad. 'Be careful in here,' he says, and opens it for you.

The Bunker is a vast cavern with an arched concrete ceiling held up by reinforced-steel ribs. Racks of weapons – knives, pistols and machine guns – line one wall. Bays made of scorched sandbags sit opposite. Sealed glass box rooms provide private labs for delicate experiments, and parked in front of you is a line of gleaming sports cars.

People in lab coats are milling about, carrying clipboards and wearing ear defenders. 'Looks like the perfect place to hide a bomb,' you remark.

'Yes. And there's a way we can find it,' Bennet says, pointing to a camera in the corner of the ceiling. 'It takes a photo each morning as a daily record for the experiments and tests, in case something goes wrong. Let's look at the photos from the last two days and see if we can spot any differences that could relate to the bomb.'

If you spotted that:

- **The machine guns have disappeared,** turn to **chapter 30**
- **The briefcase has moved,** turn to **chapter 20**

28

THE HEAT TEST

'Our analysts down in the Bunker have an ultraviolet light,' Bennet says. 'But there's not much call for an iron in this place, I'm afraid.'

You think for a moment. 'We just need something hot . . . Let's try matches,' you say, pulling a box of them out of your satchel.

Bennet nods, encouraging you.

You strike one and hold the sheet of notepaper over it, being careful not to set it on fire. As the flame warms the page, a message written in orange juice gradually turns brown and reveals itself . . .

Turn to **chapter 43**

29

SEMPER OCCULTUS

You tap the code into the keyboard and the door clicks open. Room 34 is bare and empty, except for a wooden-topped table standing in the centre and a wicker waste basket on the floor. There isn't even a chair.

You look around. The walls are empty too – there are no shelves or marks left by long-standing pictures.

You look in the waste basket. Balled up in the bottom is a tangled mess of thin brown plastic strips. They could be nothing, but something tells you they're important.

You take the basket back to Bennet and Madame Silvana. 'I found this,' you say, and empty the pieces on to the long table.

They both look astounded.

'They've been removed from an audio cassette and cut up,' Bennet says, and starts delicately pulling the bundle apart.

'Well done, Arlo, once they're unravelled and

stuck back together, we can get a transcript of what's on them and find out if we have a new lead,' Madame Silvana says.

'Can you do that?' you ask.

Bennet smiles and says, 'Our technicians can do anything.'

Twenty minutes later a technician in a lab coat arrives carrying a transcription of what was on the tape.

'OK,' Bennet says, looking at the words on a strip of paper. 'Now, if we can work out which order the pieces of tape originally came in, we'll know what was recorded on the tape, which could give us a clue about what's going on.

SIS ARE | THE BOMB

MUST BE DESTROYED

SET | ON RED ALERT

TO EXPLODE

THE WHOLE BUILDING

After a few minutes of rearranging the sections of the transcript you find two coherent messages that could've been on the tape.

A. SIS ARE | ON RED ALERT | SET | THE BOMB | TO EXPLODE | THE WHOLE BUILDING | MUST BE DESTROYED

B. SIS ARE | SET | TO EXPLODE | THE WHOLE BUILDING | ON RED ALERT | THE BOMB | MUST BE DESTROYED

If you think the original message is:

- **Message A**, turn to **chapter 10**
- **Message B**, turn to **chapter 31**

30

THE MACHINE GUNS HAVE DISAPPEARED

'It's the machine guns,' you say, pointing to the image. 'They've gone!'

'I see, but why would a bomber want machine guns?' Bennet says, sounding confused.

'I don't know,' you reply, 'but they must have a reason. Where would they take them?'

Bennet looks around. 'The back doors are the most obvious option, I suppose. They lead to the car park.'

'Let's go,' you say, and head off.

A hydraulic motor opens the doors with a loud hum. The car park is rain-soaked and grey. You spot a black van parked a short distance away.

'Does that belong to the SIS?' you ask.

Bennet shrugs. 'It might. We have a lot of unmarked vans and cars. Our operatives use them for missions all the time.'

'OK. Let's see if they've got the machine guns,' you say, and march up to the van. 'Can you open up, please?' you demand and bang your fist on the side door. 'We're looking for a hacker who's stealing secrets, killing people and threatening to blow up the building.'

The door opens to reveal two women and a pile of machine guns. 'We wouldn't know anything about all that,' one of them says.

'Well, apart from the bit about killing people,' adds her accomplice, and they both open fire on you and Bennet.

THE END

31

MESSAGE B

'The bomb must be destroyed?' Bennet says as a frown settles on his forehead. 'What bomb?'

Madame Silvana looks away. 'There are a lot of secrets in this building, Bennet,' she says. 'My immediate concern is *how* this hacker discovered that we have a bomb here.'

'You keep bombs here?' you ask, sounding alarmed.

'This is a secret intelligence facility,' Madame Silvana explains. 'We don't just hold secrets here. We develop things from the intel our operatives gather from the countries we spy on. And yes, that includes making new kinds of bombs.'

Bennet confirms this with a solemn nod.

'So what do we do?' you ask.

Madame Silvana turns to you. 'Good question. Go back to Room Thirty-Four and see if you can find any other messages we missed. While you do that, I'll order a check of our weapons inventory for missing bombs.'

You spend the next hour searching the room but

you don't find anything that sheds light on their plan.

As the tea lady wheels in her trolley to serve afternoon tea, an explosion that's hotter than hellfire rips through the building, instantly melting every steel girder and hurling every brick and slab of concrete half a mile into the sky.

Anyone within five miles of the blast feels the quake. The mushroom cloud it leaves is visible from twenty miles away, and every electrical circuit in the county is sent into meltdown.

The crew deployed to investigate the blast never return. And as soon as the government realize the magnitude of the explosion and the devastation it caused, they declare the site a no-go area for the next fifty years.

THE END

32

SECURITY BOX 7184

You hurriedly do the sums and add up the numbers in your detective's journal. 'It's box 7184. I'm sure of it!' you say, after double-checking the numbers.

'Good boy!' the Boss says and claps a hand on your shoulder.

The young lad hurriedly finds security box 7184 and rips it open with the crowbar.

'Are we happy?' the wrestler man asks as the young lad pulls out a wad of envelopes and hands them to the Boss, who checks them over.

'Yeah, we're happy. Good work, boys!' the Boss says, looking around, and a smile stretches across his grizzled face. 'That was a proper team effort.'

You breathe a sigh of relief and turn to go and get help for Bennet.

'Not so fast, young man. Where do you think you're going?' the wrestler man asks and grabs your arm in a crushing grip.

'You said, if I helped you, you'd let me get help for my friend,' you reply.

He shakes his head. 'I don't think so. What do you think, Boss?'

The grizzled villain laughs and the young lad hands him the crowbar.

You glance down at Bennet. He's in a bad way, but he'll live. It's a shame you won't.

THE END

33

THERE'S SOMETHING ABOUT ROOM 88

A concerned frown stretches across your face . . .

'What is it?' Bennet asks after a minute of staring at the plan.

'Well, according to the floorplan, Room 88 is rectangular. But now we're here, it appears to be perfectly square,' you say, pointing to your sketch.

Bennet's eyes widen as he realizes you're right.

As you work out the orientation of the room in relation to the plan, you both turn and look at the far wall, where four clocks are showing times from around the world.

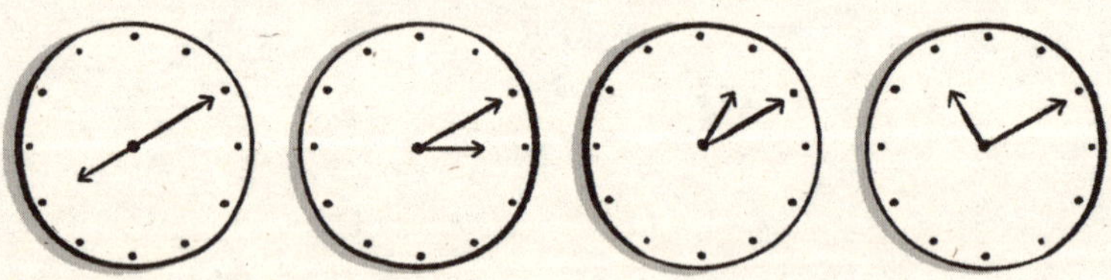

'The clocks might contain a clue,' you say, thinking out loud.

A quick glance at your watch tells you the London time is correct.

'San Francisco should be seven hours behind us,' Bennet says. 'Moscow is three hours in front and Beijing is five hours in front of Moscow.'

Use your skills of deduction to decide which clock you should investigate.

If you decide to investigate the clock for:

- **San Francisco**, turn to **chapter 41**
- **London**, turn to **chapter 21**
- **Moscow**, turn to **chapter 39**
- **Beijing**, turn to **chapter 35**

34

CODE

01000100 - 01000101 - 0110100 - 01001111
- 01001110 - 01000001 - 01110100 - 01000101

'This has got to be worth a try!' you say.

'So long as you're sure,' Bennet says with a note of doubt as you start entering the code into the keypad in the side of the warhead. 'It's not just our lives in your hands; it's the lives of everyone in this building and the members of the public we're supposed to keep safe. They're all depending on us.'

As you type in the last number, the LED screen flashes red.

'That doesn't look good,' you say, and turn to Bennet.

His face is as white as a sheet, and the screen suddenly flashes as it counts down . . . 3 . . . 2 . . .

You want to say sorry to Bennet, and to everyone else you've let down, but it's too late.

There's no time left for that, or anything else.

In a blinding flash, the warhead sets off a chain

reaction that instantly incinerates the pair of you and the entire building. Every brick, concrete slab and steel support is blown apart. Even the roof is hurled into the sky and burned to ash before it hits the ground.

The force of the blast is felt several miles away. The mushroom cloud lingers over the site for days as the shock echoes round the whole world.

THE END

35

BEIJING TIME

'Let's try this one,' you say, picking the clock set to Beijing time.

The moment you lift it off the wall the second hand starts ticking backwards . . . 3 . . . 2 . . .

You turn the clock over to find a mercury switch that's triggered by movement and wired up to about half a pound of plastic explosive. It's not nearly as powerful as a nuclear warhead, but one second later it blows the entire room apart, incinerating the walls, the net curtains, the windows, Bennet, the body lying on the floor and, of course, you.

The only thing that does survive is the false wall the clock was hanging against, and the hacker who has been hiding safely behind it all along.

As the building is evacuated and the emergency services race to the scene, the hacker strolls out of Room 88, slips unnoticed into the crowd, and simply walks away . . . With all the country's most closely guarded secrets.

THE END

36

GAS BOMB IN THE CANTEEN

Bennet leads the way to the Canteen. It's approaching lunchtime and lots of people are settling down to eat. The large room has a clamour of cutlery, china and conversation.

'How can we find a bomb in here?' Bennet asks as a sense of hopelessness settles on the situation.

You shake it off and grab an empty serving dish and a metal spoon off the kitchen counter. Then you climb onto the table and start hitting them together.

CLANK! CLANK! CLANK!

'Can I have your attention, please?' you call out as the conversations stop and everyone turns to see what the noise is all about.

'Thank you, Arlo,' Madame Silvana says, stepping in. 'We have reason to believe there could be a gas . . .' Her sentence is cut off by an explosion that rips through the floor, engulfing the Canteen, the building and everyone in it.

Every brick and shred of concrete is incinerated in a few short seconds. But you don't live to see it.

Years later the investigators conclude that the explosion was triggered by a new experimental kind of bomb that has, to date, only been used in test sites.

THE END

37

CODE

01000100 - 01000101 - 01000110
- 01010101 - 01010010 - 01000101

You type in the code and the LED screen flashes once before it shuts down.

Bennet breathes a sigh of relief. 'Well done, Arlo. You just saved a lot of lives.'

'Thanks, but we still have a hacker to catch. And the small matter of a murder to solve,' you reply.

'Of course,' Bennet says. 'Let's go take a look at the body.'

Bennet leads you to Room 88. It's a sealed perfect cube and feels confined. The body of a man wearing a worn cream linen suit is lying face down on the floor with a hunting knife in his back. Four clocks on the far end wall are ticking away the time in four cities around the world.

You crouch down beside the body and take a closer look at the man's white hair and wrinkled face, and wonder who he is and why anyone would stick a knife in his back.

'I've kept the room locked since he was found,' Bennet says. 'I'm the only person who has a key.'

'And there's no chance the body is that of our hacker?' you ask.

'No. The hacking continued after we forced the door open and found him,' Bennet replies.

'So that leaves us with two options,' you say, nodding.

If you think you should:

- **Search the body**, turn to **chapter 40**
- **Explore the room**, turn to **chapter 15**

38

LINE C

The room that connects to Line C is on the top floor, near the kitchen. As you knock and open the door, a cloud of steam billows out.

You wave the steam away and find you've arrived in a room where a lady with a peroxide perm is filling a large silver urn with boiling water.

'Hello,' she says as she notices you. 'Fancy a brew?'

'That'd be lovely,' you reply. 'I'm actually investigating a murder.'

'You must be Arlo Banks, the young puzzle-solver.' She smiles. 'I think you've gone a bit off track.'

'I guess so,' you say, slightly surprised she knows who you are.

'Not much happens round here without me knowing about it,' she says, and hands you a cup of tea.

'Thank you, you're very kind,' you reply.

'Well, we've got to look after our operatives,' she says.

'Oh, I'm not an operative,' you say, nearly choking on the tea.

'You're working on a case for the SIS. That makes you an operative,' she says with a wink. 'And from what I hear, you're a good one.'

'I don't know about that. I'm looking for a murderer and a hacker but so far all I've found is dust,' you say, casting an eye over the mess you made of your clothes crawling through the air ducts.

'Well, there aren't any hackers here,' the tea lady says.

You thank her and head back to the Telephone Exchange to take another look at the switchboard.

You stare at the phone lines and start retracing each of the wires across the board, looking for any that split off to an extension where the hacker could have been listening in.

If you can find a phone line with an extra spur, it could lead you to a room where the hacker has been gathering top-secret intelligence.

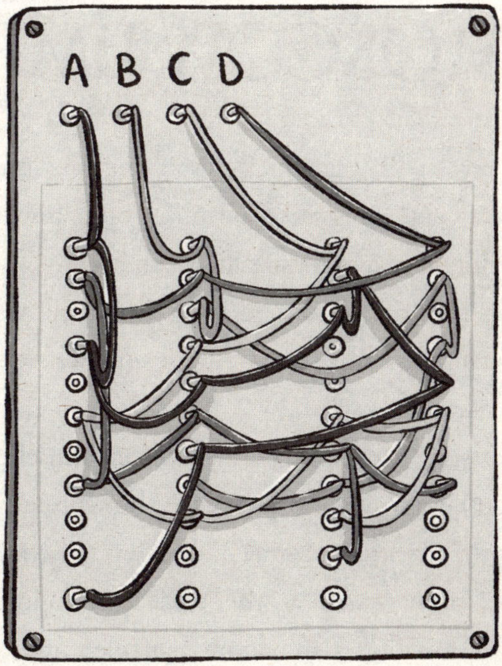

If you want to investigate the room at the end of:

- **Line A**, turn to **chapter 4**
- **Line B**, turn to **chapter 22**
- **Line D**, turn to **chapter 7**

39

MOSCOW TIME

'You reach for the clock displaying the time in Moscow, expecting it to be hung on a hook, like most clocks, but it doesn't lift off the wall.

You grip the edges and try giving it a twist. To your surprise, it turns and a motor somewhere inside the wall starts to whirr.

You step back and Bennet braces himself. 'I've worked here for over fifteen years,' he whispers, 'and this is the first time I've seen anything like this.'

You both watch as the wall retracts into the ceiling, revealing a miniature apartment. There's a bed, a desk with a computer, even a sink and a little stove. A monitor in the corner shows the live feed of the room you're in, from a surveillance camera discreetly hidden somewhere. There's also a man who's been in hiding in there for a long time.

He hurriedly grabs something from a drawer and turns on you . . .

BANG!

The moment Bennet sees the gun he pushes you to the floor and crouches down to protect you.

You both huddle there, expecting the next shot to kill you . . .

Instead, the panicked gunman makes a run for the door. Bennet grabs his legs and brings him toppling to the floor. You jump up and put all your weight on his back.

'It's all right, I've got him,' Bennet says, pulling the man's arm up behind his back. 'You go and get help.'

Ten minutes later the gunman has been led away for questioning. Bennet shakes your hand. 'Thanks, Arlo, you've been very helpful. We couldn't have caught the hacker without you.'

'What about the murder?' you ask, remembering the body in the room.

'Don't worry, we'll get to the bottom of that,' says Bennet with a smile. 'I have a feeling the hacker will be able to shed some light on it.'

And with that he shows you to a car that's waiting to take you back to your old life.

As the car pulls away, you think back to your time with Bennet and SIS, and wish you could go back and find a more successful result.

THE END

40

SEARCHING THE BODY

You start by patting down the worn linen suit. There's a handful of change in one of the trouser pockets, and a receipt for a cup of coffee and a newspaper he must've bought from a station kiosk a few days ago. You think that's everything but then you find a folded piece of notepaper that's been slipped inside the jacket's lining.

You reach in through a slit in the seam and take out the notepaper. To your total surprise, it has your name written on the front.

Bennet is as surprised as you are.

'You'd better open it,' he says.

Nerves make your hand tremble as you open the note . . .

To your disappointment, the note is blank. You turn it over to check the other side but the only visible word is, 'Arlo'.

The only other thing you get is a fleeting scent of something that smells a bit like fruity perfume.

Bennet peers over your shoulder, as intrigued to see what this is about as you are. 'It could be written in invisible ink,' he says. 'A lot of old-fashioned spies used it in case their intel was intercepted before it reached the intended recipient.'

You open your detective's journal and look up invisible ink. It tells you:

> There are two ways to reveal messages written in invisible ink. Which method you use is dictated by the type of ink the message has been written in. Ultraviolet light will reveal UV-ink whereas the heat of an iron will expose a message written in citrus juice.

If you think you should try:

- **Heat**, turn to **chapter 28**
- **Ultraviolet light**, turn to **chapter 23**

41

SAN FRANCISCO TIME

You lift the San Francisco clock off the wall. It's heavier than you expected, so you turn it over to check the other side. There's more to this clock than a simple mechanism and a battery. There are also a couple of wires . . . and they're connected to a hand grenade!

The blood drains from Bennet's face.

'It's all right,' you say, sounding a lot more confident than you feel. Holding your breath and taking every bit of care you can, you reach into your satchel and feel around inside.

'Are you sure about this?' Bennet asks as you pull out your Swiss army knife and select the wire cutters. 'Let's just think this through.'

You nod in agreement.

If you think you should:

- **Cut the black wire**, turn to **chapter 42**
- **Cut the white wire**, turn to **chapter 44**
- **Do absolutely nothing**, turn to **chapter 26**

42

BLACK WIRE

'It's all right, this'll work,' you say, and carefully hook the black wire in between the open blades of the wire cutters.

'I really hope you're right,' Bennet whispers, and draws a deep, nervous breath.

You close the blades round the wire and – clip – you cut it in two. Nothing happens and you both let out sighs of relief.

But a moment later you realize the clock is still ticking . . .

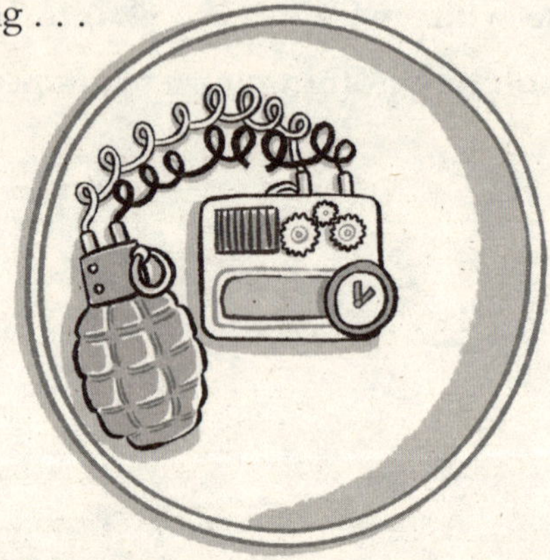

If you think you should:

- **Cut the white wire**, turn to **chapter 44**
- **Do absolutely nothing**, turn to **chapter 26**

43

THE PROFESSOR'S LAST LETTER

Dear Arlo,

Congratulations. If you're reading this, you have come a very long way and really are a remarkable puzzle-solver.

Sadly, it also means that you have found my body.

I'm sorry we never got to meet in person. I couldn't risk revealing myself to the world, but I can tell you now that I have spent much of my life working for the Secret Intelligence Service.

During my time here I have seen many things. But now I see a world that's changing and becoming more dangerous and more complex. Our enemies are developing new tactics and fighting with new methods. Intelligence is vital to keeping the world and its people safe. If stolen, it can become a powerful weapon.

And if our intel is destroyed, the country can't defend itself. This is why it must be protected.

But our methods of protecting it will soon be obsolete. This is why I set up the competition that brought you to my attention and sent you on your travels. I'm pleased to say you have succeeded admirably.

Well done!

That said, your work is not over yet. I believe your puzzle-solving skills will be a vital part of protecting our country in the future, and you must always be ready for anything. If you can solve one last puzzle, it will lead you to the start of something new . . .

Good luck!

Professor Hamatum-Sizzle.

'Arlo, I'm so sorry,' Bennet says as he reads the words that have appeared on the notepaper.

'Thanks,' you say. But the Professor's last piece of advice echoes in your head: *You must always be ready for anything.*

Puzzling thoughts turn over in your head as you gaze around the room . . . Your eyes settle on the four clocks hanging on the far wall . . .

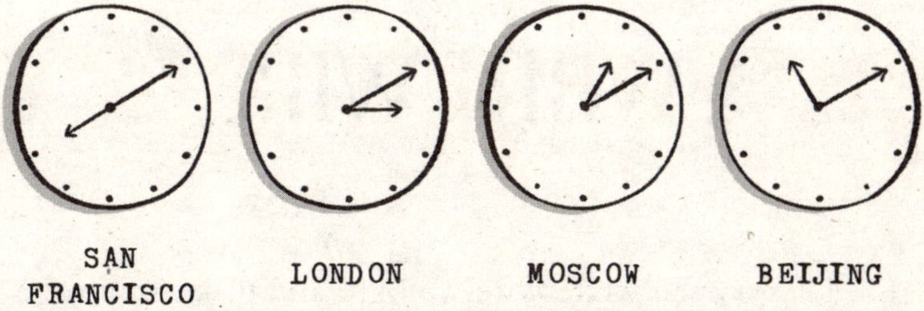

A quick glance at your watch tells you the London time is correct, but something about the clocks strikes you as odd.

'San Francisco should be seven hours behind us,' Bennet says, frowning at the time differences. 'Moscow is three in front of London and Beijing is five ahead of Moscow.'

Use your skills of deduction to decide which clock you should investigate.

If you decide to investigate the clock for:

- **San Francisco**, turn to **chapter 41**
- **London**, turn to **chapter 21**
- **Moscow**, turn to **chapter 45**
- **Beijing**, turn to **chapter 35**

44

WHITE WIRE

'Let's try the white wire,' you say, and make a move to cut it with the wire cutters. Bennet grabs your arm, but he's too slow to stop you.

It's done.

As the two severed parts of the wire come apart, there's a loud *bang!*

You instantly flinch, but you're OK. It didn't come from the grenade.

As you look around, a quizzical expression takes over your face and you realize Bennet is lying on the floor beside the body. He's been shot!

As the last breath slips from his body, your eyes widen and you try to figure out what happened.

You soon realize there's a smoking bullet hole in the wall under the clocks. You should run out of there, but against your better judgement, you peer into the hole.

There's another *bang!*

And your body drops to the floor beside Bennet.

THE END

45

IN THE NICK OF TIME

You approach the far wall and reach for the clock showing the time in Moscow. You expect it to be hung on a hook, like any other clock, but it doesn't lift off the wall.

You grip the edges of the clock and give it a twist. To your surprise, it turns and a motor inside the wall starts to whirr.

You step back and Bennet braces himself. 'I've worked here for over fifteen years,' he whispers, 'and this is the first time I've seen anything like this.'

You both watch as the wall retracts into the ceiling, revealing a dark recess. It's like a miniature apartment. There's a bed, a desk with a computer, even a sink and a little stove. A monitor in the corner shows the live feed of the room you're in, from a surveillance camera discreetly hidden somewhere. There's also a man who's been in hiding in there for a long time.

He hurriedly grabs something from a drawer and turns on you . . .

BANG!

A gun goes off and Bennet drops to the floor.

Your instincts kick in and you duck down.

BANG! BANG!

More bullets fire out of the recess as the gunman lets rip!

You flatten yourself against the floor, putting the Professor's body between you and the gunman.

BANG!

BANG!

BANG!

The sixth bullet ricochets off the concrete floor and punches a hole in the wall behind your head. You hear a couple of metallic clicks that tell you the gunman is reloading. This is your chance to escape, but if you leave Bennet, he'll become the next murder victim!

Thinking on your feet, you realize there's only one thing you can do: you grab the handle of the knife sticking out of the Professor's back and pull it out.

The tiny window of time gives you an advantage, but you only have one shot at this.

He has six.

As he aims the gun, you hurl the knife. It spins through the air – blade over handle, blade over handle.

BANG!

The bullet misses but the knife does not.

It hits the gunman in the shoulder, and the pain inflicted by the steel blade knocks him to the floor.

As he collapses, the gun falls from his hand with a clatter and spins away out of his reach.

A double dose of shock and horror cascades through your body and you stare, aghast, at the man slumped on the floor with a knife in him.

Bennet grabs the gun off the floor. His leg might be bleeding, but he can still take charge of the situation. 'Who are you?' he demands.

The man slumped on the floor looks up and laughs. 'I could tell you but it wouldn't do any good.'

'We'll see about that,' Bennet says, and cocks the gun.

The man shrugs. 'OK. But I'll warn you, once you know the truth, you can't forget it. You can't just go back to a life of happy ignorance.'

'Tell us why you killed the Professor!' you demand, getting up. 'What did he ever do to you?'

'That might be the name you know him by, but he had many names,' the man replies. 'I took him out because he uncovered my little operation here. I thought that would be enough, but the people I work for have a strict scorched-earth policy – leave nothing behind. As soon as your organization was aware of my existence, they sent an order to wipe you off the face of the earth.'

'With a nuclear bomb?' you say.

The man smiles. 'We're nothing if not true to our word.'

'Who exactly do you mean by we?' Bennet asks with a sense of dread.

'We're the Chain,' he replies, and peels back the lapel of his jacket to reveal a short metal chain pinned inside. 'We're the chain reaction, the chain of events, and one day, the chain of command.

'We're linked to everything: governments, corporations, businesses and financial institutions, mercenary armies, various secret services, terrorist groups, organized crime. Even your precious aristocracy.' He turns to you with a look in his eye that needles you. 'I heard you ran into Luigi Cabrini and Lady Hamilton.'

You're about to say something but he starts to squirm in pain.

Bennet reaches out to help him but he waves his hand away. 'Believe me, there's nothing you can do. One day you'll all be living in chains, you'll see.'

As you take in the revelation, your eyes look down at part of the Professor's letter:

. . . now I see a world that's changing and becoming more dangerous and more complex. Our enemies are developing new tactics and fighting with new methods . . .

. . . This is why it must be protected.

An hour later you're sitting in the Board Room with Bennet. His wound has been dressed and he has a brand-new pair of crutches.

Madame Silvana is listening to a phone call. She thanks the caller and hangs up. 'It appears our hacker will survive,' she says.

A huge sense of relief washes over you.

'Our operatives will continue to question him as soon as he's conscious,' she continues.

'What about the organization he works for: the Chain?' you ask.

'They're something we must deal with,' Madame Silvana replies.

'Madame, if you'll permit me . . .' Bennet says.

Madame Silvana gives him a polite nod.

'. . . Arlo has proved to be incredibly helpful in this case. And, with respect, I think the Professor wasn't just on to something, regarding the Chain. His plan to recruit someone with an original approach to puzzle-solving was a very good one. We should consider inviting Arlo to join the SIS permanently.' He turns to you and says, 'We won't just put your puzzle-solving skills to good use; you'll be helping us keep the country safe. It'll also honour the Professor.'

Madame Silvana presses her fingertips together with a thoughtful look.

This feels like an unbelievable opportunity.

You're about to tell Madame Silvana how much you'd like the chance to work for Bennet, her and the SIS, but before you can open your mouth, she says, 'Arlo, I am inclined to agree with Bennet and the Professor, but first I'd like you to solve one more puzzle.'

'Of course,' you reply, sounding eager and ready for anything.

Madame Silvana smiles. 'That's good, but I warn you, it's not straightforward.'

46

ONE MORE PUZZLE

Madame Silvana reaches into her jacket and pulls out a sheet of paper. She slides it across the table to you.

On one side is the alphabet in Morse Code. On the other is a page of ruled lines.

'Is that it?' you ask.

Madame Silvana gives you a knowing smile and says, 'Arlo, everything you need to solve this puzzle is in your hands. So all I can do is wish you the very best of luck.'

A	● ▬	N	▬ ●
B	▬ ● ● ●	O	▬ ▬ ▬
C	▬ ● ▬ ●	P	● ▬ ▬ ●
D	▬ ● ●	Q	▬ ▬ ● ▬
E	●	R	● ▬ ●
F	● ● ▬ ●	S	● ● ●
G	▬ ▬ ●	T	▬
H	● ● ● ●	U	● ● ▬
I	● ●	V	● ● ● ▬
J	● ▬ ▬ ▬	W	● ▬ ▬
K	▬ ● ▬	X	▬ ● ● ▬
L	● ▬ ● ●	Y	▬ ● ▬ ▬
M	▬ ▬	Z	▬ ▬ ● ●

,	▬ ▬ ● ● ▬ ▬
.	● ▬ ● ▬ ● ▬
!	▬ ● ▬ ● ▬ ▬
[SPACE]	● ● ● ● ● ● ●

SOLUTIONS: DEATH ON THE TRACKS

Chapter 4: The Cori Cambrian Conundrum

This puzzle is a race against time. In under a minute you must find the wire that has a complete circuit. The clever bomb maker has added the black wire as a decoy. There's a missing loop in there. So you must cut the stripy wire before it's too late!

Chapter 6: Climbing on to the Roof

There are two routes across the roof of carriage No. 3 that will bring you to the skylight or air vents at the far end, and follow a sequence of numbers. But there are two number sequences! Because this is carriage No.3, the sequence that goes up in threes will guide you to the ladder that will help you get down safely. The sequence that goes up in sixes might be quicker, but you should be careful, as hurrying often leads to putting a foot wrong.

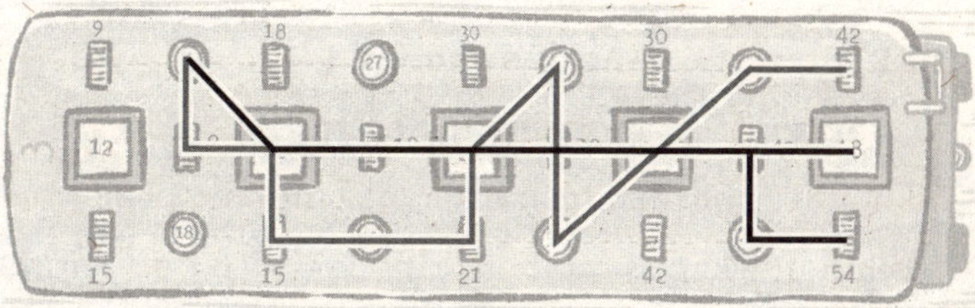

Chapter 8: The Locked Door

Chapter 39: One Locked Door Leads to Another . . .

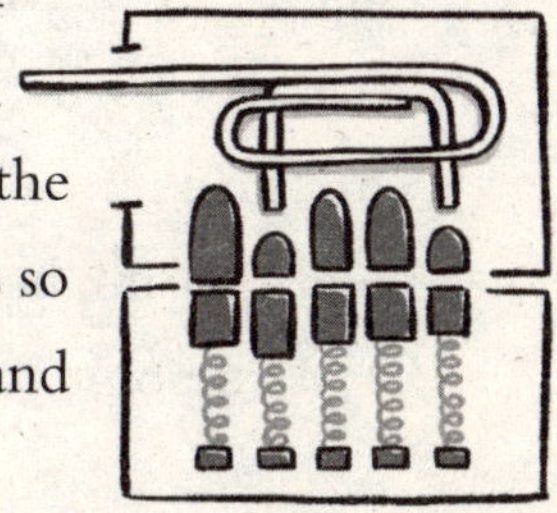

Combining the paperclip and the staple will push down the five pins so they line up inside the tumbler and enable you to open the lock.

Chapter 12: Marco Cabrini of Cabin No. 12

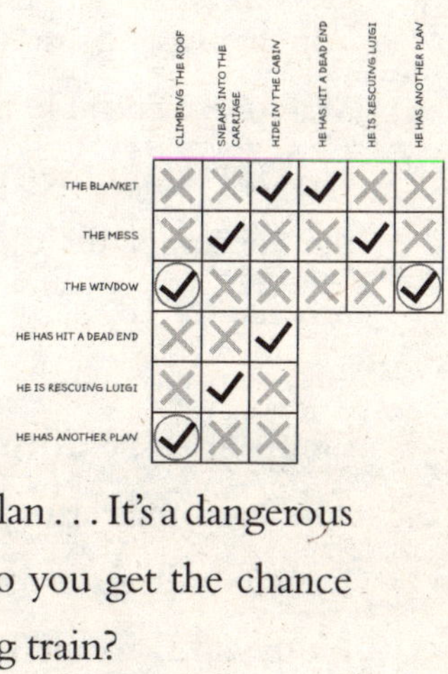

Since Marco Cabrini couldn't have slipped past you and the air in the cabin is cool and fresh, all the clues point you in the unlikely direction that he escaped to the roof through the window so he could climb on the roof because he has another plan . . . It's a dangerous lead to follow, but how often do you get the chance to run along the top of a moving train?

Chapter 16: Examine the Gun

Chapter 40: Fingerprint Section D

The sliver of fingerprint that matches the print you found in Marco's cabin is Print B, which came from the trigger.

Chapter 18: The Letter

'Marco Cabrini', 'Ric Rami Bacon' and 'Cori Cambrian' are all anagrams of 'Ari Cabin Corm'. Luigi Cabrini, however, is mentioned in chapter 1 as a clue to point you towards Marco Cabrini.

Chapter 23: The Dropped Clue

Chapter 21: Mable C. Dinki of Cabin No.21

You're looking for the name Marco Cabrini. He is in cabin No. 12. The other names on the passenger list can be seen on chapter 18.

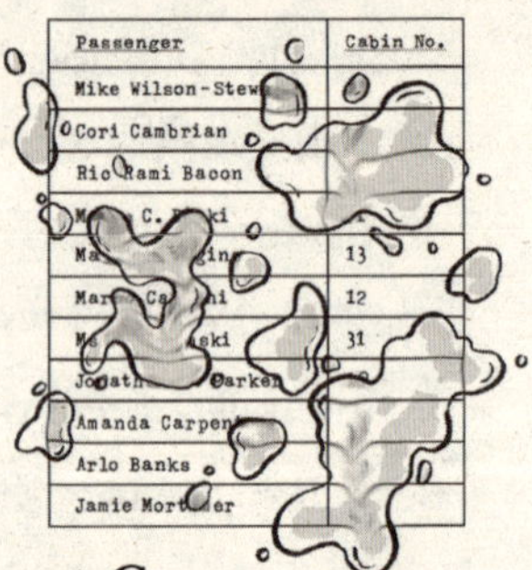

Chapter 24: Footprints Suspect C

The loop that leads to loose end A is free, so if you were to pull it, the rope would come undone. Pulling loose end B would create an even tighter knot.

Chapter 25: Marco Cabrini

Of course, it could've been any of the three suspects, but as it says through the middle of the word search, IT IS THE MAN IN THE RAINCOAT.

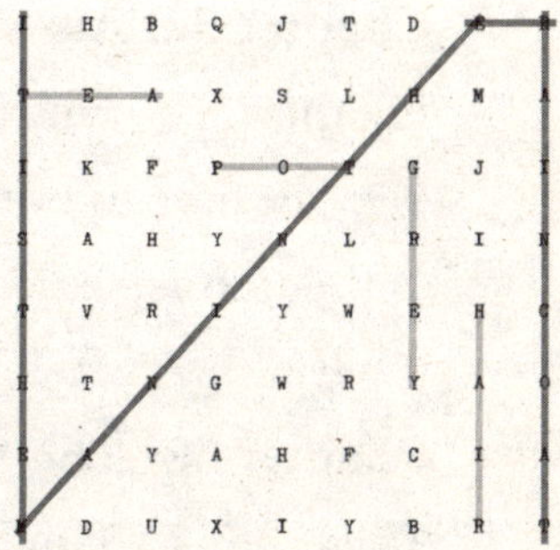

Chapter 30: The Man in the Raincoat

Chapter 14: The Toilet

Every door is different. Cabin 11's door is slightly open. Cabin 12's door is shut. Cabin 13 has a DO NOT DISTURB sign on the handle, and Cabin 14's door has a lock that you usually find on a toilet door, because . . . it's a toilet. Cabin 12 is the door you should open because Marco Cabrini slammed it just before you arrived on the scene.

Chapter 32: Air Vent 42

All the pipes will fit into place. You just have to overlap a couple of them to reconnect the boiler.

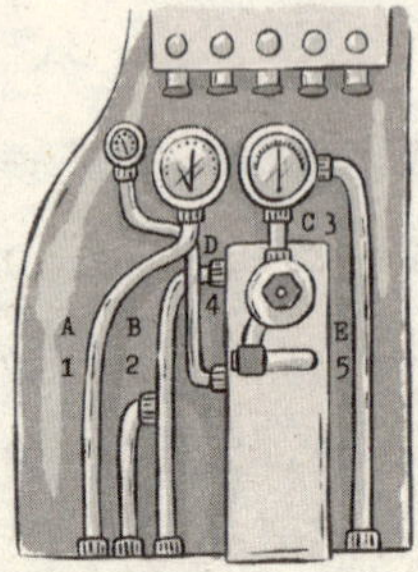

Chapter 38: The Stripy Wire Smoker

There are two differences here. In the left-hand picture, the door is slightly open and a hand is emerging. In the right-hand picture, someone is running away.

The difference you spot is the one to follow. If you spot both differences, the extra clue to help you choose between them is the fact Marco has the habit of running away from the scene of the crime, so you should follow him…

Chapter 41: Finding Footprints

All three sets of prints head off the page. There is a clue in the text that tells you Marco Cabrini has always been light on his feet and they head straight out of there, so you should follow footprints C.

Chapter 44: Footprints Suspect A

To call the emergency services, you must dial 'eyeball, eyeball, heart'. This makes sense of the clue 'finding love will save you'. 'Home is where the heart is' is there to mislead you!

SOLUTIONS: THE SCARAB'S REVENGE

Chapter 3: The Gun

They might seem like just a list, but the first letter of each line spells: POISON.

> Pure and simple.
> Oddly effective.
> It isn't for everyone.
> Soon it might be, but it isn't.
> Once is enough.
> Never going back.

Chapter 4: Shock on the Sundeck

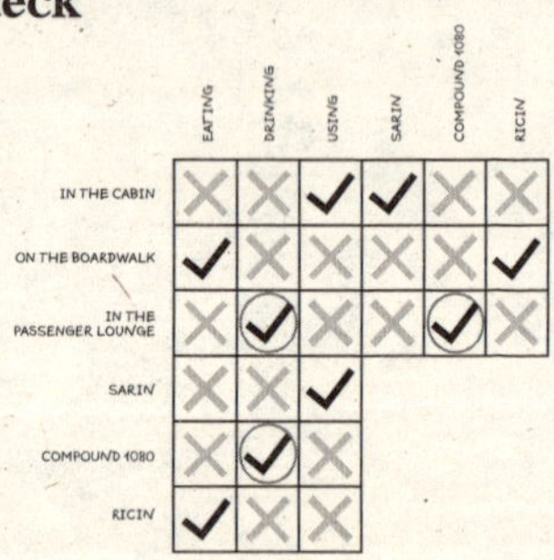

Since Miss Patti was fine when you met her in the bar and nothing in her cabin smelt poisonous or had been tampered with, all the clues indicate that she was poisoned in the Passenger Lounge bar with Compound 1080, which is water soluble so it must've been in something she drank.

Chapter 5: The Games Room

You can move any of the black pieces, but to win the game, simply use your knight to take the white queen. However, it would be wise not to upset your opponent. To spare their blushes simply move one of your pawns.

Chapter 7: The Death of Clara

Clara circled the letters: B, R, I, D, G, E and R. Since the letter I is circled twice, it's safe to conclude that, in her confusion, Clara was trying to identify the Brigadier rather than Bridget. She will also have seen someone in the Brigadier's trench coat before they fled the scene.

Chapter 17: The Killing in the Cabin

The gunshot was the last thing you and everyone else heard. If Miss Patti had been strangled, it would've happened before she was shot, and she would've been poisoned sometime before then. For the poison to have time to work and make her foam at the mouth, it would've had to have been given to her before either of the other methods killed her. So the poison is the murder weapon.

Chapter 26: The Towels in the Cabin

There is an extra corner sticking out from under towel A, which is the corner of a note from Abasi.

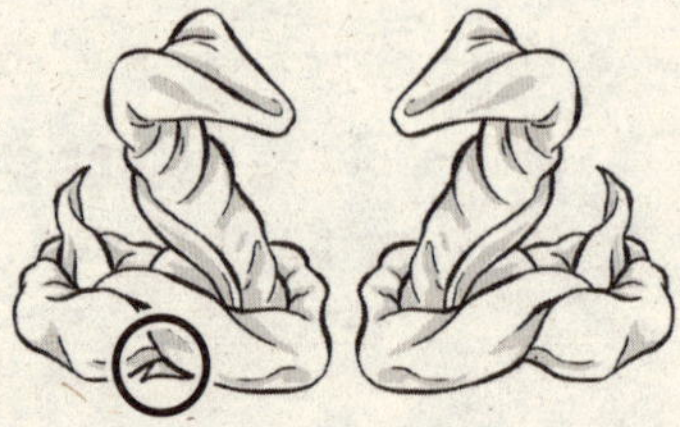

Chapter 29: The Passenger Lounge

Chapter 30: The Clever Little Spot Test

If you piece together the broken glass you will make four bottles. However, none of them make the port bottle, so you can conclude that the port bottle has been taken!

Chapter 32: The Valley of the Kings

Chapter 14: Another Block

Removing blocks A, B or C will trigger another rockfall, but removing block A will cause the blocks above it to fall and leave a space that's big enough for you to escape through.

Chapter 33: Suspect Maze Chase

The maze will take you to A, B or C. Since this is an ancient temple, what you find in each of these destinations is anyone's guess, so it's best to follow the clue in the text and avoid doubling back or retracing your steps so you find your way in and out again and solve the case.

Chapter 34: The Tyre Track Test

Chapter 35: Tyre Track Option C

The tracks will either take you round in circles or lead you out of the car park. Set B are your best bet to get you on your way.

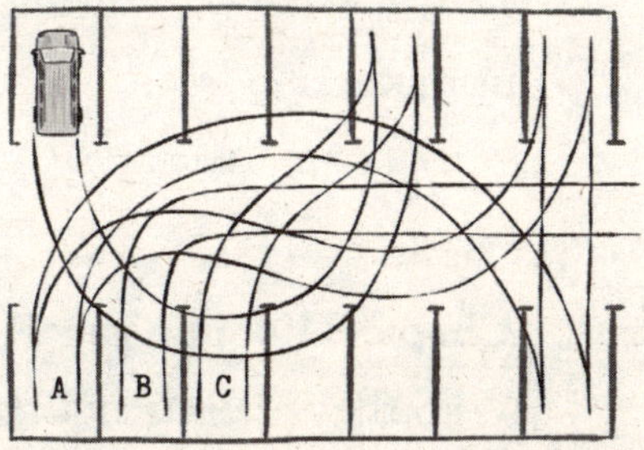

Chapter 36: Dinner Poisoning

The port bottle begins its journey in the centre and goes to Gerald. It then travels across the table to the Brigadier before moving left to Bridget then Constance and back to the centre. It then goes to Clara and to you, before returning to the centre.

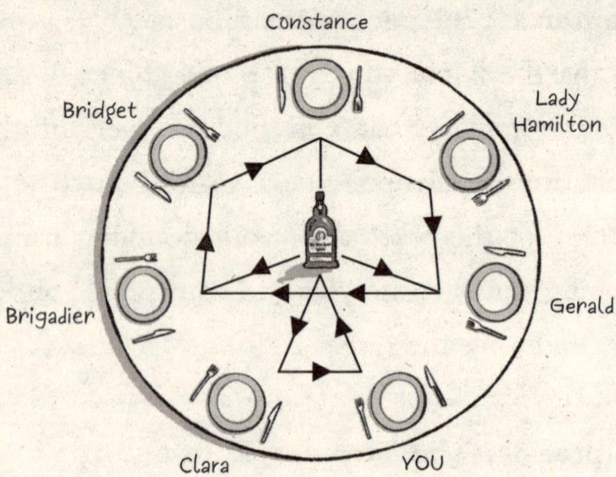

Bonus answer: Only read once you've caught the killer! The deciding clues are that the routes of travel form an arrow that points to Constance.

Chapter 40: The Big Reveal

Who the Scarab is and how they are exacting their revenge is a real mystery, but a great detective like you shouldn't need any help working out whodunnit!

SOLUTIONS: THE HIDDEN HACKER

Chapter 3: The Lead on the Hacker

These numbers of the rooms the hacker has visited are from the prime numbers sequence. The odd one out is 34. You might have guessed it was 101, because all the rest are less than 100, but it's the number that isn't part of the prime number sequence that we are looking for here.

Chapter 8: Room 34

Chapter 6: September October

The answer is *Semper Occultus*, the motto of the SIS, which Arlo notices as he arrives in the building. It means 'Always Secret'.

SEMPER OCCULTUS

Chapter 10: Message A

The roof is the only place where a remote control will work and a bomb placed here won't destroy the whole building. And since the sprinklers will extinguish any fires, all the clues indicate that the hacker has set an explosive device in the Bunker triggered by a timer. And it's a big one!

	A PHONE LINE	A REMOTE CONTROL	A TIMER	THE CANTEEN	THE BUNKER	THE TELEPHONE EXCHANGE
AN EXPLOSIVE	✗	✗	✓	✗	✓	✗
AN INCENDIARY	✓	✗	✗	✗	✗	✓
A GAS BOMB	✗	✓	✗	✓	✗	✗
THE CANTEEN	✗	✓	✗			
THE BUNKER	✗	✗	✓			
THE TELEPHONE EXCHANGE	✓	✗	✗			

Chapter 15: Exploring Room 88

All the rooms on the floorplan are rectangular, and the sketch of Room 88 shows that it is square. A most intriguing discrepancy.

Chapter 17: Exit C

Chapter 38: Line C

Starting at the top, if you follow the path of Line D through all the extensions it is plugged into, you will find that it eventually splits in two, creating an extra extension that will take you to the room where the hacker has been listening

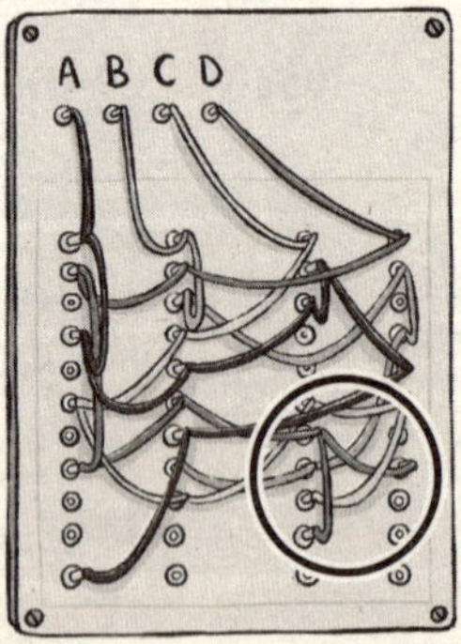

Chapter 19: The Air Duct Maze

Outcomes A, B and C are all accessible; it's just a question of where you end up. Try to avoid getting stuck inside.

Chapter 20: The Briefcase Has Moved

The clue here is the size of the hot spot. It would stand to reason that a big bomb would have the larger hot spot, but that wouldn't be the case *before* the bomb goes off. And a large hot spot in the Canteen might not be a bomb?

Chapter 22: Line B

The numbers in the boxes come from the numbers 1 to 16 cubed (e.g. 2 x 2 x 2 = 8, 3 x 3 x 3 = 27, and so on). The missing numbers have been added to the grid below. 1 + 343 + 2744 + 4096 = 7184. So the answer, and the security box you're looking for, is number 7184.

1	8	27	64
125	216	343	512
729	1000	1331	1728
2195	2744	3375	4096

Chapter 24: The Hot Spot in the Basement

Code

01000100 - 01000101 - 01000110
- 01010101 - 01010010 - 01000101

translates as **DEFUSE**

Code

01000100 - 01000101 - 01110100 - 01001111
- 01001110 - 01000001 - 01110100 - 01000101

translates as **DETONATE**

It really is as simple as that!

Chapter 27: The Bomb in the Bunker

The machine guns are missing and the briefcase has moved. While the guns might appear to be more dangerous, they wouldn't be much use to someone who's planning to blow up the building, so you should investigate the briefcase.

Chapter 29: Semper Occultus

The answer here comes from which of the two coherent messages sounds the most like an urgent order: (The alternative version is also missing a small word!)

SIS ARE | ON RED ALERT

SET | THE BOMB | TO EXPLODE

THE WHOLE BUILDING | MUST BE DESTROYED

Chapter 33: There's Something About Room 88

Chapter 43: The Professor's Last Letter

Use the information to work out what the times on each of the clocks should be. Since you know that the London time is correct, you will discover that the time on the Moscow clock is wrong. As an extra clue, it hasn't moved since the last time you were in Room 88.

Chapter 40: Searching the Body

Your detective's journal tells you that heat will expose messages written in citrus juice. The smell of oranges you got when you opened the letter was a clue, upon which you should base your decision.

Chapter 41: San Francisco Time

Chapter 42: Black Wire

Both the black and white wires are decoys. To detonate the hand grenade you must pull out the pin, so your best option is to do nothing . . . unless you find yourself in a situation where you have no choice.

Chapter 46: One More Puzzle

To solve this, you must find the Morse Code symbols hidden throughout the book and write the translations on the lined page to reveal a hidden message. Sorry, but that's all the help you're getting with this one. Good luck!

ACKNOWLEDGEMENTS

Every author's journey to publication is different. Mine has been long and sometimes puzzling, so it's fitting that this book is full of possibilities, dead ends and a few endings where things works out.

This book wouldn't have worked out without the help of a lot of truly wonderful people, and to each and every one of you I owe an unrepayable debt of thanks.

To Gill McLay and everyone at the Bath Literary Agency, thanks for all your help and support. You've always believed in me, and I treasure working with you – thank you.

To Tom Rawlinson, my editor, thank you for championing this project from the beginning. And to the whole team at Puffin, thank you, you're the best!

To Emily Gazzard, Nina Farrall, Steve Bell, Claire Henry and Julia Gibbs, thank you for your help. Brad Schreiber deserves a special thank you. I don't know where I'd be without all your editorial advice.

Special thanks to Giles Hales-Tooke, Andrew

Finch, and Ewan Lamont, who literally got off his death bed to buy my books; thank you, I'll never forget you, buddy. And to all my friends who've asked, 'So, how's the writing going?' There are far too many of you to list here, but thank you all.

I'd also like to thank my parents for encouraging me to write, and reading to me when I was little and too lazy to do it for myself.

And lastly, to my wife, Maria. None of my books would be possible without you. I love our life together and I owe all my happiness to you. Thank you.

ABOUT THE AUTHOR

Paul Westmoreland has been a professional writer for over 25 years, creating award-winning adverts for TV, cinema, radio and digital campaigns. He is now a full-time children's author and, as well as coming up with fiendish puzzle and mystery books, he is the writer behind the spooky *Rudy* series for young readers, which was first published in 2023.